# THE
# TRUTH
# ADVANTAGE

# THE
# TRUTH
# ADVANTAGE

*The 7 Keys to a Happy
and Fulfilling Life*

## LIS WIEHL
### WITH BRUCE LITTLEFIELD

John Wiley & Sons, Inc.

Published by John Wiley & Sons, Inc., Hoboken, New Jersey
Published simultaneously in Canada

For general information about our other products and services, please contact our Customer Care Department within the United States at (800) 762-2974, outside the United States at (317) 572-3993 or fax (317) 572-4002.

Wiley also publishes its books in a variety of electronic formats and by print-on-demand. Some content that appears in standard print versions of this book may not be available in other formats. For more information about Wiley products, visit us at www.wiley.com.

ISBN 978-1-118-02515-4 (cloth); ISBN 978-1-118-15636-0 (ebk);
ISBN 978-1-118-15637-7 (ebk); ISBN 978-1-118-15638-4 (ebk)

Printed in the United States of America

10  9  8  7  6  5  4  3  2  1

*For my FBI agent dad, Richard Wiehl,*
*the human lie detector*

# Contents

PART FOUR

# Unlocking the Advantage

# Acknowledgments

Good people live the truth, and I had the privilege to talk to, meet, and work with a lot of them for this book.

I want to thank my co-author Bruce Littlefield—a person anyone would want to have as a friend. He's a talent, a joy to work with, and someone that I'm glad is in my life.

I'm honored by my friends and colleagues who trusted me with their stories and by all the people from across America who took time to take the American Truth Survey, without their honesty and frankness this book would not have been possible. Thanks, too, to all of the amazing "truth experts" who graciously shared their expertise, including psychiatrist Dr. Dale Archer, former CIA special investigator Dan Crum, FBI Agent William Daly, deception and technology professor Dr. Jeffrey Hancock, communication expert Dr. Mark Knapp, Director of the Institute of Child Study Dr. Kang Lee, public relations professional Colleen McCarthy, relationship authority Dr. Margaret Paul, and body language expert Tonya Reiman.

Thanks to brilliant editorial assistant Karina Grudnikov, who contributed so many great ideas, and my Internet savvy intern, Ben Levine, who set up the American Truth Survey.

Our literary agent Todd Shuster, at Zachary Shuster Harmsworth, believed in this project from the beginning, and is not only a great agent, but also a gentleman and a friend. The team at Wiley Publishing was terrific to work with, including Executive Editor Tom Miller, who asked smart questions and gave great advice, Senior Production Editor Richard DeLorenzo, copyeditor Patricia Waldygo, Senior Editorial Assistant Jorge Amaral, Senior Marketing Manager Laura Cusack, and publicists Mike Onorato and Matt Smollon. Without their efforts, this book would not be in your hands.

Thank you, Bill O'Reilly, Roger Ailes, and Dianne Brandi. I feel incredibly honored to have your encouragement and support. And special thanks to Deirdre Imus, who instantly "got" The Truth Advantage message.

Mom, thank you for your unwavering belief in writing a book about telling the truth. You once said that life isn't fair, but if we tell the truth to others and, most importantly, to ourselves, we will navigate the course. You have been my role model all along.

And lastly, to my kids, Dani and Jacob: I couldn't be a prouder mom. When I look at the two of you, I see what my mom said is true. I am excited to see you navigate your own course (with the tiniest of meddling from me along the way).

# PART ONE

# Let's Be Honest

*In a time of universal deceit, telling the truth is a revolutionary act.*

—GEORGE ORWELL

# CHAPTER 1

# Get The Truth Advantage

*No legacy is so rich as honesty.*

—SHAKESPEARE

This book will help you become a better, happier, and more powerful person by using only one tool—the truth.

When you tell the truth and can obtain the truth from others, you are manifesting your best qualities, both inwardly and outwardly. You are someone others want to have around. You are someone whom people listen to, learn from, and look to for strength. You respect yourself, and others respect you. In short, your life is happier.

Through dealing with hundreds of juries and analyzing news and newsmakers, I've learned that liars get caught, and the truth always wins out. If you look closely at those around you, you'll realize that in your everyday interactions with friends, family, and colleagues, when you tell the truth, people like you, respect you, and are truthful with you in return. If you're being honest—whether in business or your personal life—you are both attractive and persuasive. People want to know you and help you more; by being truthful and understanding of the truths that others tell you, you forge deep, powerful, life-changing bonds and relationships.

How, then, does truth help you rise above? Why is telling the truth easier and more powerful than not doing so? Mark Twain put it simply, "If you tell the truth, you don't have to remember anything." The truth helps you inside and out: inside, because you avoid the inner turmoil produced by lying; and in your outer life, through trusting relationships with others. The truth not only shows on your face, it manifests in your life. You only have to tell the truth once, but you have to remember and retell a lie forever.

According to Daniel Langleben, a psychiatrist at the University of Pennsylvania, lying requires far more effort than truth telling. His years of research in brain-scan detection have proved that, in order to tell a lie, the brain first has to *stop* itself from telling the truth. After that, it creates the deception and then catalogs it. The more you lie, the harder your brain works, and the more tired you become. Your brain becomes a juggler with too many balls in the air. Or, more specifically, concocting lies weighs you down and makes everything in life more difficult.

There's wisdom in the old proverb that it's easier to simply tell the truth. The truth lifts the weight off your shoulders. It gives you a clear conscience, a sharpened focus, and a boost in power that no one can take away. Simply put, the truth will set you free.

A lie, on the other hand, is a mean moving target. Just ask anyone who has ever been caught telling a lie or who has fallen victim to one. That's probably all of us.

You'll be hard-pressed to find someone who has never told a lie. We all lie in fairly regular and predictable ways. For instance, according to the research of Robert S. Feldman, a professor of psychology and the interim dean of the College of

Social and Behavioral Sciences at the University of Massachu-setts, people meeting for the first time lie to each other at a rate of two to three times for every ten minutes of conversation. That's a whole lot of lying.

But why do we lie? Lying is certainly an elusive combina-tion of human traits. "Of course, they're real." "It fits you per-fectly." "I have a headache." As you'll discover, though, lying is also a learned survival technique. We lie to build ourselves up and because we think it will protect us from pain and suffering. That's the mistake. It does neither.

Whether big or small, lies are eventually exposed, and liars end up with egg on their faces. If you're sixty-three, but your online dating profile says you're forty-two, sooner or later, someone you date will realize the math doesn't add up. From then on, will this person be able to trust anything else you say? If your résumé states that you graduated Phi Beta Kappa with a 4.0 GPA from Harvard, it takes a human resources person only a few clicks of the computer mouse to check whether you are on the list of people who actually did.

And if you think your extramarital dalliances won't catch up with you, you're wrong. Having served as counsel for the Democrats during the impeachment of President Bill Clinton, I've seen the dire consequences of big-time fibbing up close. It's not a pretty picture. Whether it's a sitting president, a famous athlete such as Tiger Woods, a public figure such as presidential candidate John Edwards, or simply one of the scores of adults across the globe who is caught in an adulterous situation every day, covering up such sexual shenanigans almost always back-fires. You will leave a trail—whether physical or emotional—and eventually will be caught, if not by your significant other, then certainly by your conscience.

My dad is an ex-FBI agent. Nothing gets past him. I grew up in a house with a living, breathing lie detector and learned quickly as a child that telling the truth was always the best way to go. If you told a lie, you'd eventually get caught. My dad always said that if you don't get caught by someone else, you'll get caught by yourself.

Here's why I am telling you this: I'm a mom. My kids need the truth from me, and I need it from them. I'm a friend. My friends expect the truth from me, and I expect it from them. Who wants a dishonest friend? I'm a lawyer. Okay, I know what you're thinking. Although I was trained in the tools and wordplay of the courtroom, I realized that in trials, the best results saw truth tellers redeemed and the liars sent away, rebuffed and punished. I earned the distinction as one of the top trial lawyers in the country by always telling the truth to my clients, my witnesses, and my jurors. In doing so, I never lost a case.

I told my witnesses and crime victims what I had learned growing up: that if they were truthful with themselves and with me, they'd sail through. And they did. The truth removed the bumps and the potholes from the road. I watched firsthand as those who swore to tell the whole truth and nothing but the truth—and did so—came out winners. Those who didn't? Well, many went to jail.

Today, as the legal analyst for the Fox News Channel, I witness almost daily the self-imploding nature of deception, how one simple lie can quickly destroy the reputation, the career, and the life of someone at the top of his game. At my core, I'm motivated to stop the devastation that I've seen lies cause to the liar and those around him and to herald the transformative power that the truth wields. I've seen this power in my own life. I rely on the truth to explain a diversity of complex issues and to stand strong against some of the biggest know-it-alls in the business, people who are paid to disagree with me.

In addition to my own experience—in scenarios that range from the courtroom to the classroom, from my living room to the television studio—I consulted a group of international experts, individuals who have made careers out of studying the truth, why we lie, and how to detect deception. I also surveyed and interviewed more than three hundred people for my American Truth Survey, who answered very personal questions about their truth telling, their lies, and their lives. These experts and the survey helped illuminate and enlighten my search for the truth. As a result, I discovered the positive, life-changing consequences of telling the truth.

Yet your goal isn't just winning an argument or gaining superiority; rather, it's making an earnest effort to become more forthright, kind, and true to your word. I've experienced amazing benefits in my own life from following these straightforward techniques. I hope that The Truth Advantage will free you from worry, lift your spirits, and help you and your loved ones become happy, successful, and fulfilled in every way.

This book will help you improve every aspect of your life:

- **In business,** the truth yields long-term associations, contributes to a better work environment, and translates into a higher income.

- **In romance,** the truth makes for stronger, livelier relationships and adds incredible spice.

- **In parenting**, the truth enables you to connect deeply with your children and to protect, respect, and guide them toward successful, happy lives.

- **With friends,** the truth makes you forever honored, trusted, and remembered fondly.

The seven keys to truthfulness, which we'll explore in the book, will produce benefits in a wide range of situations, from the boardroom to the bedroom. In addition to real-life examples, I will also share information and stories from psychologists, relationship experts, body language specialists, and media stars to demonstrate how each key works in practice—and how you can use these seven keys to be consistently direct and forthright and enrich your interactions with others.

The Truth Advantage demonstrates how being truthful will bring about positive changes in your life and will help you become a significantly more humane, loving, and compassionate person. It will also teach you how to help others be truthful with you. You will learn the best way to appropriately and thoughtfully encourage everyone you encounter—friends, colleagues, and family—to be fully honest.

The Truth Advantage will empower you with your own personal lie detector—a truth-seeking missile that finds the heat of someone's lies and distortions. You'll learn the secrets of how psychiatrists, private investigators, and trial attorneys, as well as other "people readers," get to the truth. The truth is written on the face, heard in the voice, and seen in the tell-tale signs we leave behind. This book will teach you the questions to ask, the things to look for, and the techniques professionals in the truth-detecting business use to dig for facts and unearth the truth.

The point is not to try to catch friends and loved ones in lies but, rather, to cultivate truthful and mutually respectful relationships. The Truth Advantage will help you convey authenticity, caring, and understanding so that your friends, colleagues, and loved ones never feel compelled to lie to you again. Encouraging others to be truthful with you will give you peace of mind. In turn, the person who learns to be truthful with you will build a noble character and rock-solid self-confidence. Finally, that truthfulness will foster better bonds, increased trust, and deeper personal commitments with everyone you know.

Being truthful will bring you greater contentment. You'll be more self-confident, feel less weight on your shoulders, and have greater clarity about yourself and your values. In short, you'll enjoy a seamless life and leave behind a proud, distinguished legacy.

The fundamental benefits of truth telling will enable you to become a person of character and strength in these volatile times, which will benefit not only you, but also the people you care about. Following these simple techniques will take you to the next level in your career and family life and will carry you well into your future.

Living in such a fast-paced, egocentric, and money-driven era, what do we most want to hear? What do we most want to know? Whom do we most want to be with? What makes us feel at ease and comfortable?

We all want to know that we are living with loving people we can trust. It is in our nature to seek honesty and feel attracted to people we can believe in. We each want a solid anchor in this turbulent world. We all hope to be considered strong and virtuous. This book will reveal the benefits that living truthfully will bring to your life.

# CHAPTER 2

# The American Truth Survey

*Anything more than the truth would be too much.*

—ROBERT FROST

Let's start with the bad news. We all lie. It's become a normal part of everyday existence. We're not bad people. We've simply found a not-so-nice method to make ourselves look better, to keep ourselves out of trouble, and to alleviate our pain. Unfortunately, these lies do the reverse. In the end, we don't look better. We get into trouble, and we cause ourselves more grief.

Why? Because the truth always comes out.

Before I began writing this book, I decided to survey Americans from all walks of life about their thoughts on the truth— how they perceive it, how they deliver it, and how they get it from others. What I discovered is that people give a lot more thought to why they lie and what they lie about than they do to wondering why they don't simply tell the truth in the first place.

Remember when George Costanza on *Seinfeld* insisted, "It's not a lie if you believe it?" That's become the way of the world for a lot of people. Even if we don't believe this, it seems that we all find many ways to validate our lies and reassure ourselves that such inventions are okay and excusable. For example, the survey found that people justify their lies with everything from "It makes a story more interesting" to "It was necessary to cover up what I should have done." When it comes to lying, we tend to surprise even ourselves.

# The Questions

The survey consisted of questions and multiple-choice answers. In addition to the suggested answers, each question also allowed the participant to mark "Other (please specify)" or to provide a comment. Many people used the comment section to ask questions or provide elaborate and well-thought-out validations for their answers.

During the course of the survey and numerous interviews, many of the lies sounded very familiar to me. Do any of the following statements ring a bell for you?

- "My battery went dead."
- "I had no cell coverage."
- "I'm fine."
- "I'll call you."
- "We're just friends."
- "Let's get together soon!"
- "My alarm clock never went off."
- "The bus/train/plane was late."
- "The traffic was horrible."
- "I don't have any money."

- "I never watch TV."
- "I ran five miles today."
- "It will be ready in five minutes."
- "I'll be ready in five minutes."
- "Yum!"
- "I love it!"

I had heard (and said) a few of those lines before. Perhaps one or more of them sounds familiar to you, too. I had to chuckle at fifty-nine-year-old Floridian Bonnie's question in the comments section: "Does biting my tongue count as a lie?" Well, I suppose not, but ouch, that must hurt.

*Question #1:*
*How many times today did you tell a lie or at least avoid telling the entire truth to someone?*

    a.  0
    b.  1
    c.  2
    d.  3–5
    e.  6 or more.

Of those who responded, 25 percent said they had lied at least once that day, while only 2 percent said they had lied six or more times. (Joe, a thirty-four-year-old from California, admitted, "If someone hooked me up to a lie detector, it might overheat.")

Yet 59 percent of those surveyed said they had not lied that day at all! "Not me." "No way, never!" As their survey answers later revealed, however, that doesn't mean they don't lie at all. The day of the survey just happened to be a non-lying day. As we say on TV, "Back with more on that in a moment."

Before going any further,

—ASK YOURSELF—
**Have you lied today?**

*Question #2:*

*If you could ask someone anything and get the absolute truth, who would that be?*

   a.  Spouse/partner
   b.  Child
   c.  Boss/colleague
   d.  Parent
   e.  Friend.

Please list a specific question for this person.

There were two leading answers: 30 percent said they'd want to know the truth from a spouse or a partner and 27 percent said from their child. In addition, 13 percent of respondents said they'd want to know something from a friend, while 9 percent said bosses and colleagues and 16 percent would want to know something from their parents.

Some examples of specific questions included

- "Does my wife really love me?"

- "Is my husband faithful?"

- "Is my son engaging in teen sex?"

- "Was I born out of wedlock?"

- "Is my boss going to ever give me the promotion?"

- "Is my daughter doing anything I should know about?"

What struck me about these percentages was that 30 percent of the participants seem to be saying they have doubts about their spouses or partners, whether it be something they've done or something they've said, and 27 percent have similar misgivings about their children. That's a lot of mistrust of some very important people.

It was also interesting to note that many of the questions were about sex. Many individuals were concerned with fidelity in their own relationships, whereas others worried about their children's sexual lives. A lot of people noted that they always wondered how many sexual partners their spouses had really had.

Liz, a forty-eight-year-old woman from Arkansas, told a story about how she finally learned the truth about her husband's experiences and used it to her advantage. "After twenty-five years of marriage," she wrote, "I got my husband to admit I wasn't his 'first.' It was after his high school reunion, and I met a woman who said she had dated him in high school. I tricked her. I said, 'He told me you were his first.' She replied, 'Oh, I don't think I was his first. He got around.' Instead of getting mad, I decided to use the information to spice up our bedroom."

—ASK YOURSELF—
**Whom do you want to know the truth from?**
**What do you want to know?**

*Question #3:*
*What is the reason behind most of your lies?*
  a. Preserving self-esteem
  b. Other people's feelings
  c. Covering mistakes
  d. Other (please specify).

An astounding 62 percent of the people said they lie because of other people's feelings, 11 percent said "self-esteem," 15 percent said "covering mistakes," and 12 percent said "other."

Some examples of specifics:

- "To avoid conflict and arguments over things that are not the business of others."
- "To minimize financial loss on a project."
- "I only tell 'Does this make me look fat?' lies."
- "To make a story more interesting."

- "So that people don't have to see my poor self-esteem or judge my actions in a poor light."
- "By omission when talking to my liberal/progressive friends."
- "To get my kids to behave."
- "Everyone lies on their online dating profiles. I have to in order to keep up."
- "To keep him from yelling at me when I spend money on something he doesn't agree with."
- "I don't lie, but maybe I will spin things to cover for someone who made an honest error."
- "I don't think being vague or elusive is a lie."
- "So people don't ask more questions."

Those last two struck me. From my courtroom experience, I know that if you're being vague or elusive, people will instantly question what you're saying—whether judge, jury, or your best friend. And if you think you are telling a lie so that people won't ask you more questions, don't fool yourself! Ask any attorney who has ever questioned a witness on the stand—a lie actually yields more questions. Whether spoken or unspoken, if you lie, it is guaranteed to make people have more questions, not less.

What I found interesting in analyzing the survey is that roughly three out of four people think their lies are to protect or spare other people's feelings. As you'll see later in the book, this has been proved false. We lie for ourselves. We might think we're lying to protect other people, but, in most circumstances, we're in actuality lying to make ourselves feel better, or appear to be better people, even though we don't realize it or aren't willing to admit it.

Claire, a thirty-seven-year-old married woman from New York, admitted that she didn't quite know why she was lying. She couldn't figure it out herself. She was stumped. "I recently found myself lying at my aunt's funeral," she wrote. "I remembered her and spoke about her fondly when, in fact, I don't remember her fondly at all! I held the family party line when I should have said, 'I remember her using a vine from her garden to switch my bare behind when I asked for a second cookie. I remember her slapping a man in a grocery store. I remember her locking me out of the house until bedtime.'"

Perhaps this untruth was Claire's way of keeping peace in the family. Or maybe she was following the "Don't speak ill of the dead" mantra. She could have even been subconsciously repressing or erasing those bad memories, attempting to take her own hurt and anger out of the equation. I'm betting that the other family members would have been supportive, even in agreement, or some perhaps would have collapsed in stitches if Claire had said what was really on her mind: "Aunt Bitty was a piece of work!"

Chad, a twenty-seven-year-old man from Montana, was very clear about why he did something, but he suggested that it really wasn't a lie. He wrote to say that when he was in high school, rather than being honest with his friends that his family lacked status and wealth, he created a new job title for his father. "I told people in school that my dad was the general manager at a hotel when he was actually a janitor." Chad then suggested that telling other people how "great" his family was "might not be a lie but really an exaggeration."

Let's get real. You and I both know that people were probably aware of Chad's father's profession. Most likely, no one cared whether he was a janitor or a manager. The person they really cared about was Chad. Who is Chad? It's only human nature to note the discrepancy and then ask ourselves, "Is that guy honest or dishonest?"

Seriously, think about your classmates in school. Wasn't it generally known what people's parents did, whose uncle got arrested for breaking into the liquor store, which students got good grades, and which kids were in the "slower class"? Those who were not honest about their own situations were probably less liked, not for the fact that those situations made them better or worse, but because they weren't truthful about their set of circumstances, about their lives . . . about themselves.

The same is true with adults. If someone knows you, he or she is probably aware of many truths about you. Why not acknowledge that you're aware of them, too?

— ASK YOURSELF —
**What is the reason behind most of your lies?**

*Question #4:*
*Whom do you tend to lie to the most?*

    a.  Parents
    b.  Coworkers
    c.  Friends
    d.  Spouse/partner
    e.  Other (please specify).

Whom do you think the survey participants professed to lying to the most? The results might shock you.

The sad souls who are lied to the most are actually our friends, at 39 percent! Is that because we talk to our friends more often or because they are easy targets? "I lie to friends most often in the sense that I often stretch the truth when I'm asked to get together with someone," explained Kim, a twenty-three-year-old woman in Tennessee. "If it's a bad night or I just want to hang out with my husband, I sometimes exaggerate a smaller obligation I have in order to make the night seem busier. That way, I don't have to tell the person, 'I just don't feel like hanging out with you today.'"

Katherine, a sixty-four-year-old woman in Illinois, said she recently had a breakthrough with a friend. "For years, I've been telling her that I like her choices and tastes in artwork, cooking, and fashion," she wrote. "My friend finally looked at me one day and said, 'You really don't like my style, do you?' I said, 'Well, no. I don't.' She didn't change her tastes, and I didn't change mine, but I believe by finally calling me out, her honesty truly made us better friends."

In formulating question 4, I left off "child" as one of the choices—maybe I'd like to personally think that I don't lie to my children—but 21 percent of the respondents wrote it in! In third place, 20 percent said they lied the most to coworkers. Parents were lied to most often by 12 percent of the people, and 4 percent of the people who chose "Other" said they lied the most to "debt collectors." (I left that one out, too!)

So, we admit lying most often to those we are closest to! Yet our web of deceit doesn't stop there. On the "Other" lists were lies to bosses, neighbors, professors, bill collectors, and even a yoga instructor! You get the picture. We'll lie to anyone about anything!

#### —ASK YOURSELF—
#### Whom do you tend to lie to the most?

*Question #5:*
*As a child, did you ever catch your parents lying while teaching you not to lie? Looking back on it now, did your parents lie to you, but you didn't realize it until you grew up?*

Only 28 percent of the people said no. (And some of the no's were really yes's.) The rest of the respondents, a little more than 70 percent, said yes! their parents lied to them. Here are some of their memories:

- "Yes. They would tell someone on the phone a lie because they didn't want to do something with that person at the time. They called these 'white lies.'"

- "Yes. They told me there was Santa and the Easter Bunny, and I was sad when I found out otherwise."

- "No. Never observed a lie, other than my dad allowing me to charge personal gas on his company's account."

- "Yes. My mom was guilty of lies of omission. 'Don't tell your Dad we spent all this money. Don't volunteer it.'"

- "Yes. My mother told me an elaborate story about my birth certificate, saying it was destroyed in a fire at the hospital. Not so, I found it online. I think I may have been illegitimate, even though both parents were listed."

- "Yes. My mother had us lie about our ages to get cheaper prices at dinner or the movies. I think I was 'twelve' until I was almost seventeen."

- "Yes. There are a lot of skeletons in my mother's closet."

Beverly, a forty-eight-year-old woman from New York, took the time to get something off her chest. "My mother would always pretend that things were nice in our house, that my dad wasn't a selfish man who still is at the age of seventy-nine. She was also prone to sneaking the bottle of vodka after my father went to bed, to hide her pain over no one wanting to visit her because of his bully-like behavior. Even though she pretended, everyone knew."

One thirty-five-year-old man from Vermont felt that his parents had lied to others but were actually too honest with their children. "My parents were always sharing things with my siblings and me, to the point of sharing too much. They'd tell us about financial struggles, marital struggles, and, on several occasions, even about their sex life. They would do this, and then we'd watch them lie to others—friends, neighbors, and even my grandparents."

All of this will certainly make you think twice now about your actions in front of your children, won't it? These answers certainly got me thinking.

— ASK YOURSELF—
## Did your parents lie to you?

*Question #6:*
*What do you tend to lie about the most?*
   a.  Work
   b.  Dating and sex
   c.  Academic success
   d.  Age.

"I'm kind of shocked at your multiple choices," a thirty-two-year-old woman from South Carolina scolded me. "You must not know any liars. If you told any of these lies, they would quickly catch up with you. I only lie to spare someone's feelings. If a friend who looks horrible because she just had a baby says, 'I look fat and exhausted," I may say something like, 'No! You look fantastic for someone who just had a baby.'"

Perhaps she's right. Several people pointed out that they thought, here again, my answer options missed the mark, and after reading the responses, I realized they were right!

Only 7 percent of those responding chose "work." I thought that "work" was a possible answer, because of the many lies we've heard in the news recently concerning everything from embezzlement to fraud, from pyramid schemes to professional athletes. It seems that neither Ponzi schemers, used-car salesmen nor sports stars responded to the survey.

It made me happy to see that only 6 percent said that they lied about their "academic success." And I was shocked that a mere 4 percent said they lied about their age! Which tells me that only twelve of my friends in the TV business responded. A joke, a joke! But seriously, have we finally reached a place where people are being honest about their age? If so, bravo!

Only 8 percent said they lied about dating and sex, yet it is interesting to note that "online," "Facebook," and "dating sites" appeared frequently among the answers, accounting for 22 percent of the responses. I would call that "dating and sex," but apparently, America doesn't think so! I have often heard people embellish or discreetly hide things about their dating and sex lives, particularly while on dates. When I crafted the survey, a friend had just told me that her boyfriend had lied about how much money he makes. She discovered this six months into the relationship. She's very successful in her own right, so it wasn't the lack of a bank account that worried her. She was concerned about his honesty. Could she trust him? She's now having second thoughts about whether this is the man she wants to marry.

America didn't agree with my multiple-choice selections. Instead, it was "Other" that captured the day, claiming 78 percent of the total! And, yes, I did leave out some big lies. I suppose we lie about so much that it's hard to break it down into a menu of four simple choices.

According to the survey, a lot of people lie about money. In fact, money was an answer for 20 percent of those who responded.

- "Money."
- "Money."
- "Money."
- "Spending money."
- "How much things cost."
- "I lie to my husband about the money I spend."

The rest of the "Other" answers included such lies as

- "I lie when someone is pressing me for a response that I'm not prepared to give."
- "I tell people 'I'm busy' all of the time just because I really don't want to see them."

- "I tell my son he's talented at some things, even though he's not, to encourage him."
- "That I don't watch much TV."
- "To get out of a tight spot."
- "To save someone from getting hurt."
- "Status of work tasks."
- "Little things."
- "When I'm going to visit Mom."
- "Conflicts in my schedule. Doesn't everyone in the workplace do that?"
- "I give out the wrong name and phone number a lot."
- "What I did on my sick day."
- "Spock taught us that omission is not a lie."

Also, many people mentioned the "white lie" as an important tool in life. Jackie, a thirty-five-year-old woman from Washington, D.C., wrote, "I think small white lies are the social glue that holds society and friendships together, and I don't necessarily try to avoid them." We'll discuss this belief and other similar "white lies" later in the book.

Jake, a twenty-four-year-old man in New York, said he couldn't say only one thing and took the opportunity to explain that he thinks he has a chronic lying problem. "I'm not sure why I lie, but I do often," he wrote. "I've read the signs of a compulsive liar, and I guess I agree that I lie most to protect myself. I began lying to my parents about things like homework and then began to lie more and more to get out of things. I now lie to my girlfriend about the silliest things, like telling her I have a present for her when I don't or saying I got a promotion at work when I didn't. I really hate this part of me."

— ASK YOURSELF —
**What do you lie about the most?**

*Question #7:*
*Do you remember the first lie you ever told? If so, how old were you and what did you lie about? Please elaborate.*

I remember my first lie. When I was eight years old, like many children, I wanted a pet very badly and begged my mom and dad for a cat or a dog. Both of my parents thought I wasn't old enough to take on such a big responsibility. One winter day another third-grader brought a litter of kittens to school, and I asked for the black one with a white nose. On the way home with my kitty, I suddenly realized that I needed to concoct a lie about the kitten. So, I stuck her in a hole in the hill, turned around, spotted her, and picked her up. I got home with the kitten, and my mother immediately demanded, "Where did you get that cat?"

"I found her," I replied.

"Where?" my mom asked.

"She was in a hole on the way home. She didn't have a collar, and it's cold and snowing outside. Can I keep her?"

"Kiwi" was a part of our family for years, but my telltale heart always beat a little louder when I thought about not being truthful. A couple of years ago, I asked Mom if she remembered the story about my finding Kiwi in a hole. She said she did. Then I asked her whether she'd believed me, and she said, "Of course not, Lis. You're not a very good liar."

In this childhood question, I wanted to ferret out whether others (besides me) had early childhood memories of lying. Many people—80 percent—said that they did remember a childhood lie. Here is a sample of some of those lies:

- "I told my mom that the neighbors had messed up the playroom. That was the first sin I confessed at confession."

- "I denied doing something that I actually did. I don't remember exactly what it was, but I remember my dad lining us all up to see who did it, and my sister started crying and said she did it. I'll never forget how she took the fall for me."

- "When I was six years old, I lied to my parents when a friend told them I used foul language."

- "In third grade, I changed my report card from an unsatisfactory 'U' to a satisfactory 'S' in red and swore to my mom that the teacher had changed it."

- "I don't remember my first lie, but I do remember the one that taught me not to lie. When I was nine years old, I cheated on my math homework and then lied about it. My parents had only one punishment for me: 'We are so disappointed in you.'"

- "When I was eight years old, I lied to my mom about taking money out of her purse."

- "I was a participant in a lie about a teacher that hurt her very much. I've regretted it ever since, and my biggest regret is that I never was brave enough as an adult to apologize."

- "I stole a piece of candy and lied to my dad about it. What a mistake!"

This question also seemed to be an opportunity for a few people to get lies off their chests, to release themselves from long-harbored childhood lies. Interestingly, two lies specifically involved fire. Scott, a forty-year-old man in Minnesota, wrote, "When I was young, I started a fire in our garage. I blamed it on the neighbor's kid. His dad whipped him with a belt, and my dad would never let him back in our yard. I still feel horrible every time I think of it." And Julia, a twenty-one-year old woman in Delaware, wrote, "When I was eleven, my stepsister and I were bored, so we started setting Monopoly money on fire in the house. We told my parents it was an accident, but after a bit of time, I started to feel bad, so I told my dad the truth. He yelled at me and spanked me. I hadn't liked lying in the first place, but I really didn't want to after that. My dad had always known that I was a girl who told the truth, and when I didn't, it hurt me because I felt as if I'd lost his trust."

The answers to the childhood question proved one thing to me: lies, especially big ones, tend to stick with us even after many years go by. We carry lies with us, cluttering up our minds and weighing us down with guilt.

—ASK YOURSELF—
**Do you remember your first lie?**

*Question #8:*
*Would you say that most of your lies have led to more positive or negative outcomes?*

I am glad to report that the majority of the people—55 percent—thought that lying resulted in a negative outcome, but I was saddened to discover that 45 percent thought that their lies had actually contributed to a positive outcome. Hopefully, these are the people who believed that "white lies" contributed to the betterment of society. Probably not, though. When I read the responses, I realized that 45 percent of the people might be kidding themselves.

Here's what some of those participants who think lying has a positive effect on their lives said:

- "Lying keeps me calm at work."
- "Lies keep things status quo."
- "I think my lies help keep the peace."
- "Lying buys me time."
- "I may feel terrible, but sparing someone's feelings is positive."
- "I spin things to help someone out, not to hurt someone."
- "I rarely get caught. I think I'm a very good liar."

Yet it was the other 55 percent who brought the real effects to light:

- "Positive . . . until you get caught."
- "A lie is never positive."
- "I tend to dwell on my lies, and that makes me feel horrible. But I still do it."
- "Deceit will always result in bad karma."
- "It puts stress on me and makes it difficult for me to communicate when I have to remember to keep my lies straight."
- "Lying is never good. Not only do you feel guilty, but you usually get found out."
- "How could losing someone's trust be positive?"
- "I suffer because of the guilt my lies cause, and I have to bear the burden of my actions."

Many people alluded to something that we'll discuss later in the book: that, generally, lies always come to light. Jen, a forty-six-year-old woman in New York, explained why she thought lies were a waste of time and effort. "Sometimes a lie protects someone else, but that's rare. The rest of the time they have a negative effect on your life because the truth eventually comes out, especially when you're trying to cover your tracks. Friend: 'What did you do last Thursday?' Me: 'Nothing.' Friend: 'So why did you tell me you were busy?' Oops, I forgot I'd said that. Then I had to deal with the fallout and the fact she'd caught me in a lie. Wouldn't it have just been easier for me to say in the first place, 'I just want to stay home tonight and kick up my feet.'"

Yet it was Laurel, a sixty-two-year-old woman in Georgia, who got to the heart of the matter. She wrote, "My dad taught me a Bible verse as a child, and I will never forget it: 'Numbers 32: Be sure your sin will find you out.' It has always proved true." As you'll see, the copious amounts of research on the subject suggest that your lies do indeed find you out.

—ASK YOURSELF—
## Do you think your lies have had a positive or negative impact?

*Question #9:*
*Have you ever been caught in a lie but still insisted you were telling the truth?*

For this question, I didn't give any space to elaborate. I simply wanted to see how many people said that they stood by their lies.

It was a virtual split: while 51 percent said no, 49 percent said yes. I wish I could do a follow-up with the 49 percent. I wonder whether they realize that sticking to a lie only makes people doubt you more and more? A lie that you never let go of creates a fissure in any relationship.

— ASK YOURSELF—
## Have you ever been caught in a lie but still insisted you were telling the truth?

The last question was simple and straightforward.

*Question #10: Do you think you can go the rest of your life without telling a lie?*

Only 8 percent of the people answered yes.

— ASK YOURSELF—
## Can you get through the rest of your life without telling a lie?

Probably not. That's why the other 92 percent of us need to learn The Truth Advantage.

# PART TWO

# The Truth about Lying

*Liar, liar, pants on fire!*

—SCHOOLYARD TAUNT

# CHAPTER 3

# Why We Lie

*Lying and stealing are next-door neighbors.*

—ARABIAN PROVERB

I know of a girl, let's call her Angie, who has had brain cancer. Twice. Angie's also had a "spot" on her lung and been pregnant twice, although she has yet to give birth. About a month ago, she announced big news: she and "Dave" were moving in together! Dave was the boyfriend whom people at work had always heard about but never seen. Dave never showed up at after-work parties because he was always busy. He'd had more than a few deaths in his family, which always seemed to coincide with times when the gang was getting together.

Angie's colleagues began to test her on the mysterious Dave. They asked more and more specific questions: "What kind of car does he drive?" "Where does he live?" They'd ask to speak to him on the phone, and even though Angie would beg him to "just say a quick hi," Dave always had to get right off the phone.

Her coworkers became annoyed and more and more suspicious that just like Angie's brain cancer, lung spot, and failed pregnancies, Dave was a big fat lie. In fact, they decided, everything out of Angie's mouth was a lie.

During one of Angie's flirty conversations with Dave, a sneaky coworker decided to call Angie's phone. It rang loudly against Angie's ear. "Oh," she quickly said. "I've been talking on and on, and the call was dropped!"

Then, the following day after a coworker shared that she had gotten engaged, Angie had a big announcement: Dave had proposed to her, too!

"Did you get a ring?" a suspicious coworker immediately asked.

"Yes!" Angie bragged. "It's a family heirloom."

For a week, Angie kept forgetting to wear the ring, making excuses each day for her absentmindedness. Then, she lost the ring! "How did you lose it?" she was immediately asked. Just as quickly, she blamed it on a crazy night of drunkenness. "Is Dave mad?" someone continued to press. She hadn't told him yet, she confessed.

These types of lies—real whoppers—had gone on for months. In fact, people finally confided to one another that they believed everything Angie said . . . to be a lie. Yet the lie that finally broke the camel's back occurred when a coworker's nephew came to visit from Ireland. The coworker had received a frantic call from her nephew, who explained that immigration officials at the airport had put him on a plane back to Ireland. His paperwork hadn't passed muster.

Angie overheard the conversation and inserted herself into the action. "Dave's uncle is in the CIA," she volunteered. "I'll get him to make a call. What airport is your nephew at? Which airline?"

So, Angie set off to have Dave's CIA uncle help an Irish kid on Aer Lingus at Newark Airport get off the plane and into the

United States. I'm sure you can see where this is going. Within minutes, Angie had told her coworker that the plane had been pulled off the runway and been brought back to the gate, while the entire terminal at Newark Airport was being closed down for this international crisis. People in the office were speechless, mouths agape, as Angie's tall tale grew taller and taller. "He is going to get a personal apology from the head of the Port Authority," she bragged, "The man is going to meet the plane now."

Like all of Angie's tales, everything about the "nephew off the plane" incident (as it came to be known) was suspect, but this time her coworkers had definitive proof that what Angie was saying wasn't true. The Irish nephew had called to say good-bye, and they'd been tracking the flight on the computer while Angie was "on the phone with the CIA." The plane was already in the air and en route to Ireland. Everyone finally decided that enough was enough. Angie's coworkers gathered around her, physically forming a circle around her cubicle.

Angie looked up, and the intervention was on.

One by one, each of her colleagues told her the dreadful truth. They all gave their honest opinion of her. "We want to like you," one person started, "but you make it impossible because you are constantly lying. Nothing you say is ever believable."

Angie protested. "I never lie," she protested. "How dare you call me a liar! I can't believe you'd say I'm lying when I'm trying to help you!" Angie burst into tears. "Why would I lie about something like that?"

"We're not sure," someone else said, "but we all think you have a serious problem."

"Angie, we really want to be friends with you," another coworker added. "Your constant lying just makes it really hard. We think you're a compulsive liar."

"I am not!" she insisted through her tears. "Give me one thing, just one thing I've lied about?"

Everyone rattled off a litany of her lies. "Your cancer." "Your car wreck." "Your figure skating championship." Then, they told her the truth. "The plane is on its way back to Ireland. Dave isn't real. You aren't engaged. You've never been pregnant. . . ."

What did Angie do?

She screamed, "You're all liars!" and stormed out of the office.

There's more to the story later in this chapter, but for now, here's the truth: If you lie on a regular basis, don't fool your-self—people know it. If you lie on a semiregular basis, people question the veracity of most of what you say. And if you lie occasionally, people notice, and they guard themselves in every conversation with you, always wondering whether the next thing out of your mouth will be a load of hooey.

One thing is certain: if you're not being truthful, people are hesitant to be close to you. So, why would anyone lie? The great philosopher Friedrich Nietzsche said, "The most common lie is that which one lies to himself; lying to others is relatively an exception."

By the time you reach the end of The Truth Advantage, you will no longer lie to yourself.

Why do we lie? Whom do we lie to? What do we lie about? And how do we learn how to lie in the first place?

The very definition of dishonesty makes gauging the amount of lying we liars do hard to track, but studies based on the Bureau of Labor Statistics and the U.S. Census suggest that most of us lie once or twice a day and deceive more than thirty people a week. Shocking, right? If you are like me, you are shaking your head and thinking, No way! I'm no liar. I always tell the truth. I, um, was just fudging a little when I told my friend earlier that my husband wasn't feeling well and that we'd have to get lunch another day. The real truth is, I was just too plain tired and didn't feel like going. Yet I didn't tell my friend that.

But why didn't I? Was it to spare her feelings? To soften the blow if she realized that something else was taking precedence over her? Did I come up with the "sick husband" excuse to make myself look like a devoted wife? And did I really think that she wouldn't be able to relate to my feelings? I'm sure she's probably as tired, too! So why wasn't I frank with my friend?

According to research, when it comes down to it, lying is actually based on how we feel about ourselves. It's our egos talking. University of Massachusetts psychologist Robert Feldman has proved it. His studies have found that we lie when we feel that our self-esteem is on the line. And, apparently, it is human nature to feel that our self-esteem is under threat on a fairly regular basis. According to his study, published in the *Journal of Basic Applied Psychology*, during the course of a ten-minute conversation with a stranger, a typical person will lie at least once and on average will utter 2.92 inaccurate things!

But wait. It gets worse.

Dr. Feldman's research suggests that we not only deceive others, but often deceive ourselves, too. We convince ourselves that we are telling the truth, even when we're not! In one of Feldman's experiments, two strangers were put in a room together and videotaped as they conversed.

After the conversation had taken place, both participants were asked whether they felt that what they had said during the exchange had been "entirely accurate." Both of them were sure that it had been. They didn't lie. They were honest. Weren't they?

Each participant was then asked to individually review the video of the conversation and identify anything that was "not entirely accurate." The playback was an eye opener.

Participants were shocked at how inaccurate they had actually been. The lies ranged from small, such as pretending to like people whom they actually disliked, to outright whoppers—for example, claiming to be the lead singer in a rock band!

Why would we feel the need to tell complete strangers such fabrications, such bald-faced inaccuracies? Dr. Feldman told *Live Science*, "We're trying not so much to impress other people but to maintain a view of ourselves that is consistent with the way they would like us to be." In other words, we are trying to be social butterflies. Not only do we want to keep the boat from rocking, but we also want to make each social situation as effortless as possible. We want to avoid ruffling feathers by being agreeable, by moving the conversation along. Yet we become so caught up in thinking about how we are being perceived by the other person that we lose ourselves in fantasy.

Whether we want to come clean about it or not, lying comes naturally to all of us humans. I'll even go so far as to say that it has sadly become an expected part of life—even legal.

In 2006, President George W. Bush signed into law the "Stolen Valor Act," which prohibited people from wearing, making, selling, or even overtly claiming they have been awarded military decorations and medals. The act made it a crime punishable by up to a year in jail to falsely claim to have received high military decorations. Why had the act become necessary? Because some people will lie about anything, even acts of honor. Can you imagine boasting about heroic deeds that you never actually performed? Well, that's what Xavier Alvarez did in 2007 at a public meeting of the Three Valleys Municipal Water District in Pomona, California.

Alvarez was convicted on criminal charges for falsely bragging that he had been awarded the Congressional Medal of Honor for his service in the United States Marine Corps. In 2011, his sentence was overturned, and the act itself was ruled unconstitutional. Chief Judge Alex Kozinski of the Ninth U.S. Circuit Court of Appeals said that the Stolen Valor Act was an unconstitutional restraint on free speech and a threat to every citizen who fibs to embellish his or her image, avoid embarrassment, or perpetuate a child's belief in Santa Claus.

In his ruling, the judge said something very telling. "Saints may always tell the truth," he wrote, "but for mortals living means lying." Living means lying! I had to read that twice. Living means lying! In a judge's ruling! Although I find it reprehensible that this man lied about being a decorated war veteran, I have to say that I agree with the judge's ruling. The Stolen Valor Act is what's known as a "content-based restriction"—its intent being the desire to curb speech about a specific topic—and, therefore, it is in violation of the First Amendment. The government does not have a compelling reason to criminalize this type of speech—*even though it is a lie*—just as the government cannot criminalize flag desecration, even though that is despicable.

"If false factual statements are unprotected," Judge Kozinski wrote, "then the government can prosecute not only the man who tells tall tales of winning the Congressional Medal of Honor, but also the J-Dater [an online dating site] who falsely claims he's Jewish or the dentist who assures you it won't hurt a bit." Perhaps the judge had read Plato, who said, "Good people do not need laws to tell them to act responsibly, while bad people will find a way around the laws."

"People are always going to have traffic accidents," communications professor Dr. Mark L. Knapp explained to me. "Does that mean the world is going to hell and people aren't following traffic regulations? Does that mean traffic regulations aren't valuable or working? Just because we have con artists and people who sometimes don't tell the truth as they know it doesn't mean we shouldn't have a guideline to tell the truth most of the time. Nor does it mean that our guideline isn't working."

In other words, you're on your own, morally, when deciding whether to lie. At the same time, your own ethics will affect how you judge liars and the lies they tell. I am reminded of what Thomas Jefferson said, "Nobody can acquire honor by doing what is wrong."

Lies and liars are as old as time. Ever since we've been able to breathe, we've been able to lie. I agree with Judge Kozinski that there are very few of us mortals (I want to say none, but I won't) who aren't guilty of telling a little lie from time to time. We don't all tell big immoral whoppers such as "I'm a decorated veteran," but we do come up with some very good ones on a regular basis. Sometimes we stretch the truth, sometimes we fib, and sometimes we say whatever it takes to save ourselves in the moment.

Tad Williams said, "We tell lies when we are afraid . . . afraid of what we don't know, afraid of what others will think, afraid of what will be found out about us. But every time we tell a lie, the thing that we fear grows stronger."

Lying comes easily for most of us. We lie to get out of something. We lie for our convenience. We lie to get our way. We lie even more to cover up our mistakes or things that we aren't really proud of. Worse still, we lie an awful lot to people we know and love the best.

How do we come to be so good at it, capable of lying and denying with such ease?

Just because it seems natural to lie, don't go blaming biology! No one is forced to lie—we learn it somewhere. So, where does the ability and the desire to fib arise from? How do we become such Pinocchios?

Well, that's what childhood is for! Research has shown that we tend to learn lying by the age of two, and, once we do, we simply don't stop. According to Po Bronson and Ashley Merryman, the authors of *NurtureShock: New Thinking about Children*, a four-year-old might tell one lie approximately every two hours and would reach one lie per hour by the age of six. As the mother of two teens, I don't even want to think about how many lies teenagers tell their parents!

According to Dr. Kang Lee, a professor at the University of Toronto who studies lying, there's nothing unusual about children lying. Kids lie. Dr. Lee told me that learning to lie is just another sign that a child is developing normally. It's not that we want to make a career out of lying or spend our entire lives doing it. It's just that we naturally figure out how to lie and begin to do so more and more often as our minds develop and we attempt to navigate the world.

Yet we parents need to remember something that Carl Jung once pointed out: "If there is anything we wish to change in the child, we should first examine it and see whether it is not something that could better be changed in ourselves."

Remember when your child stood by, as you, with your sudden cough and newly nasal tone, called out sick for work? Your child observed and noted. Remember when you said, "We won't tell Daddy we spent this money on your outfit, okay?" Your child observed and noted. Remember when you told your husband that you couldn't get the dry cleaning because you had to drive the kids to a school event? Your child observed and noted and was left wondering why there was no school event to go to.

Then, you wonder how—and might even be shocked that— your child can look at you with a straight face and chocolaty lips and say, "No, I didn't eat the chocolate." How could he be so dishonest? You can't believe it! Where would he learn that? Naughty child!

Studies, such as the work of Kang Lee, have made it quite clear that telling lies goes hand in hand with fundamental maturation. In a fascinating *Wall Street Journal* article titled, "Survival of the Fibbest: Why We Lie So Well," Shirley Wang points to studies and research on how we learn to deceive as part of the process of growing up. The studies suggest that we start lying as toddlers to get out of trouble ("I didn't break it") and to get what we want ("Mommy lets me eat candy"). We master lying by the time we're adults for "self-preservation" purposes and to make others feel better ("I love your hair!").

After spending the last fifteen years studying how lying goes through a metamorphosis as children age, why certain people are bigger fibbers, and what can be done to reduce the need to lie, Dr. Lee wants parents and teachers to realize that just because they've snared a child in an untruth, they "should not be alarmed—and their children are not going to turn out to be pathological liars." If you have a little Pinocchio living under your roof, you might be relieved to know that Dr. Lee says, "The fact that their children tell lies is a sign that they have reached a new developmental milestone."

Dr. Lee and his colleague, Dr. Victoria Talwar, have been conducting *Candid Camera*–style studies at McGill University, putting kids and teens from ages two to seventeen in a lab with hidden cameras and a temptation. Each child is enticed to lie by being instructed not to peek at a toy that's put behind his or her back—often, a plush purple Barney dinosaur. When the test giver leaves the room for a mere minute to answer a phone call, the child has sufficient time to sneak a peek at the toy.

What do you think happens?

Does the child steal a glimpse? Would you?

Well, it's all on the tape.

The research team discovered that young children experience a "tremendous" temptation to cheat. An astounding 90 percent *do* peek! Dr. Lee affirmed that adolescents and adults are also tempted in similar conditions.

When the test giver returns to the room, the children are asked whether they peeked. The study's results show that a quarter of children at age two will lie. "I didn't look," says that sweet, "innocent" little child—even though he or she did. By three years of age, 50 percent lie, and by age four, the number rises to a whopping 90 percent!

This incline continues until around age fifteen, when almost all of the "cheats" will lie about it. The good news—yes, there's some good news—is that the number of liars peaks at fifteen and starts to decline after that. By age seventeen, the number of liars drops to about 70 percent.

But still . . . 70 percent!

My theory is that "The cover-up is always worse than the crime." According to Lee and Talwar's recent research, young children frequently give themselves up verbally. When asked, "What do you think the toy is?" the children who've peeked often squeal, "Barney!" And when asked how they knew . . . um, they, um, did . . . it becomes confession time for many.

Yet around the age of five, children start to understand that giving such an answer would reveal their deception. So at this age, they make believe that they're guessing or invent better reasons for why they amazingly knew the answer. One little girl asked Dr. Lee whether she could put her hand underneath a blanket that was covering the toy before she answered the question. After feeling but not seeing the toy, she said, "It feels purple, so it's Barney."

I remember when I caught my daughter Dani in a little lie when she was about six. It was something silly, but she got in trouble with me. I told her, "Young lady, march up to your room and think about what you did!"

She turned to me and said, "I demand a lawyer." Then, she said, "Wait, you are a lawyer. I demand another lawyer. No, I demand an appeal!"

Don't tell me kids aren't listening and watching all that we do . . . from a very early age.

We are quick to learn from our mistakes. It's our innate survival mechanism. We figure out how to cover our tracks while quite young by not making the same mistake twice. We learn how to look innocent and control our mannerisms, such as not looking away when being questioned. And we learn how to make excuses.

Yet why is it that some kids lie more frequently? Is it related to a worse upbringing or not being taught noble moral values? Does it have any religious significance? You may be surprised to find out—hold onto your hat—that researchers have found that kids with higher cognitive abilities are the ones who lie the most!

There goes your pride in that "My child is an honor student!" bumper sticker.

How can this be possible? According to Dr. Shawn Christ, a neuropsychologist at the University of Missouri-Columbia, in order to lie, the truth has to be in one's mind. This involves numerous brain progressions, which incorporate several sources of information and engineer the information into a manipulative untruth. Kids who achieve higher test scores on subjects related to executive functioning have an increased propensity to lie.

What are we to do? How can we encourage our kids to be more honest? Lee and Talwar suggest that we discuss with our kids why there are rules against lying. "The time to catch a liar is before eight years of age," says Dr. Lee. Furthermore, we should point out and acknowledge when children tell the truth. Accentuate the positive to encourage more truth telling, and when they lie, point that out, too.

This brings us back to Angie, our liar in an office full of fed-up coworkers. When we last left Angie, she had stormed out of the office, angry that her friends would dare accuse her of being a compulsive liar.

Is Angie a compulsive liar? What is the difference between an everyday liar, a compulsive liar, a pathological liar, and a sociopath? And what do you do if you think someone you know—your child, your friend, your coworker, or your partner—has a chronic lying problem?

A sociopath tells his tales with no concern for others. A sociopath is oriented strictly toward personal goals and feels little emotion, which is why sociopaths can often pass lie detectors. A sociopath doesn't laugh, cry, or get angry. He tells his lies in order to get his way and does so with little or no regard for anyone else's rights or feelings. Sociopaths are often charming and charismatic and use their skills in a way that ultimately benefits them.

"The best liar is someone with no conscience," Dan Crum, the "Dating Detective," told me. "When you don't associate lying with consequences, you feel no stress about lying and show very few deceptive signs."

Remember Scott Peterson, the handsome fertilizer salesman, who was living two lives up to the time of his wife's murder? To his beautiful wife, Laci, and her family, he was a devoted husband, excitedly awaiting the birth of their son. To Amber Frey, his girlfriend, he was a world-traveling bachelor who was head-over-heels in love with her. A sociopath can convince even himself that he's right, that he's done nothing wrong. I firmly believe that O.J. Simpson has convinced himself that he did not kill his ex-wife and her friend. Sociopaths are not accountable to anyone, not even to themselves.

A pathological liar exaggerates and concocts stories with little regard or concern for other people's feelings. A pathological liar actually believes the lies he's dishing out or at least believes them the moment he's saying them. His stories are grandiose and dramatic, and he often describes how he's smarter, better looking, braver, and more interesting than he really is. Pathological liars might also lie to get sympathy, yet it is often easy to catch on to pathological liars because their stories just don't add up. I know a woman who swears that she's survived a plane crash—twice! But she doesn't want to say anything further about them because it's too much for her to handle. *Um, really? Twice?* If you ask even an innocent question in regard to a pathological liar's story, the person will feel threatened or annoyed by the question.

A compulsive liar lies out of habit. Lying is a normal way of life for him. His lying begins in early childhood. His lies are not necessarily manipulative or cunning; he's simply been lying about everything for so long that he doesn't know anything but. Lying is second nature. Compulsive liars often have low self-esteem. They frequently lie to get noticed, and they create stories in order to be the center of attention. If you're friends with a compulsive liar, you'll note that he will often repeat a story in which the basic concept remains the same, but the details change. For example, he might witness a car wreck, but it takes place in a different time or place than the last time he witnessed it. His lying is an addiction. It feels right to him. Like any behavior that provides comfort, compulsive lying can be hard to stop.

"So many of my patients are relieved when they get caught," psychiatrist Dr. Dale Archer told me. "They subconsciously orchestrate getting caught because they're ready to stop living the lie."

Any type of chronic liar needs to be helped in counseling or therapy, but mental health professionals point out that getting someone to recognize and admit to the behavior is difficult. Sadly, as with drug and alcohol addiction, many people have to hit rock bottom—losing their relationships and jobs—before they will seek help. Yet you can start the process by questioning them a little more closely on the things they say and by encouraging them that it's safe to tell you the truth.

As a trial lawyer, here's what I did with criminals: I explained that in the end, truth and honesty would earn them respect. Truth would not erase the damage they had done, but if they faced their truth head on and "came clean," the judge would show them more mercy than if they held to their lies and played out a long trial.

Charlie Brown's creator, Charles M. Schulz, once said, "Sometimes I lie awake at night, and ask, 'Where have I gone wrong?' Then a voice says to me, 'This is going to take more than one night.'" We laugh, but at the end of the day, I think we all want to feel good about ourselves, even nonsociopathic criminals. I always gained a little hope for humanity when one of these felons I was questioning looked across the table at me and said, "Yes, I did it."

---

### TRUTH ADVANTAGE DO'S AND DON'TS!

**DO** keep people honest by accentuating the positive before you gently call them on a lie.
**DON'T** enable liars to keep lying by ignoring the evidence.

---

So, what happened with Angie, our compulsive, border-line-pathological liar? The following day, she returned to work and completely ignored the previous day's drama. She acted as if everything was status quo. But her coworkers had made a pact. They all agreed that every time Angie said something questionable, the only way to help her out was with tough love. They decided that they'd simply say, "Angie, I don't believe you."

At first, "Angie, I don't believe you" was heard often in the office, and she got annoyed. Angry. Every time she heard it, she cussed. As the weeks passed, however, the frequency of Angie's lies and exaggerations began to diminish, putting her on the road to gaining The Truth Advantage. Hopefully, as she is challenged to be more honest and to avoid using lies as a way to feel good about herself, Angie will get even closer to everyone she knows. The same applies for anyone you know who is not being honest about something. Help the person be honest. Remember, we all want to feel good about ourselves.

Now, let's look at what we lie about.

## THE TRUTH ADVANTAGE CHECKUP
### *We All Live in Glass Houses*

**We're all human.**

- We need to realize that we lie for a mixed bag of reasons.
- Try to recognize where a person is coming from, the motivation behind his or her lie.
- If we understand that lying is natural, it will be easier to forgive someone who has been dishonest.

**Remember, you aren't creative enough to get away with lying.**

- Realize that people notice the lies you tell, even if they don't say anything.
- Know that if you're telling a lie, there is evidence you leave behind.
- Note that people distance themselves from liars.

**Don't blame your parents.**

- Realize that your parents are human, too.
- Know that truth and lying develop organically in us at an early age.
- Make sure to teach your children what you wish your parents had taught you.

CHAPTER 4

# What We Lie About

*The end of an ox is beef, and the end of a lie is grief.*

—AFRICAN PROVERB

While sitting in a diner recently, I overheard the man in the neighboring booth tell someone on the phone, "I can't talk right now. I'm going into a meeting." A meeting with his scrambled eggs. A relatively harmless lie, sure, but why couldn't he have just said, "I'm having breakfast. Can I call you back later?"

We lie about the simplest of things. More than once, I've walked down the street and heard someone announce on his cell phone that he was on such-and-such street and "almost there," and I'd look up at the street sign to see that he had lied about his location. He wasn't, in fact, "almost there." What kind of cockamamie reason could he have not to be truthful about his location? He was setting himself up to have to tell at least one more lie when he got there.

Why can't we simply tell the truth in the first place, even when the truth isn't easy to admit? My friends know that every year I throw a big Christmas party. It's one of my favorite times of year, and I'm always excited to share it with as many people as I can. This past holiday, however, my festive spirit got the better of me, and I realized that my guest list had grown out of control. In a moment of end-of-the-year exasperation and inspiration, I came up with a brilliant plan to make my party a little more manageable. I decided that I would invite only my closest friends with whom I had very deep emotional relationships. Many terrific friends were left off the list, but it had to be done. Given the stress I was under at the time, there was no other way to make the party happen, and my solution seemed like a good one.

A few weeks later, one of the friends who hadn't been invited confronted me about her exclusion from the guest list. She wasn't happy. It would have been easy for me to smooth over the situation with a lie and tell her that there had been some kind of mistake and that her invitation must have gotten lost in the mail, but instead I was honest (but tactful!) with her. I explained to her exactly how I'd gone about compiling the guest list. I admitted that I had felt quite exhausted recently and sadly but deliberately had decided to limit the party to a very small number of friends and family. I told her that I would love to see her in the next few weeks.

We subsequently went out and had a terrific time. Honesty really is the best policy. By coming clean and explaining myself, I saved myself the potential trouble of being caught in a lie, and it gave me the opportunity to extend an invitation for future good times with my friend. By being honest, I gained self-confidence, trust, and freedom, as well as a stronger friendship. I avoided a lie and gained The Truth Advantage.

We exaggerate. Whether bragging about the size of a fish we caught or our amazing salary, we puff up the truth because it sounds better. Kids exaggerate about their grades. Just ask them. In a study conducted at Northwestern University, students were asked to fill out a computer form asking for their academic information, such as their GPAs. Later, when researchers were permitted to look at the students' records, they found that almost half had exaggerated their average by as much as six-tenths of a point. Call it wishful thinking, if you will. Perhaps they were hoping to have those GPAs? Yet kids aren't the only ones. Adults exaggerate, too. Remember when Hillary Rodham Clinton was a candidate for president and exaggerated about sniper fire in Bosnia? That didn't do anything to help her poll numbers.

Lying is an epidemic. Lies come in all shapes and sizes. Some lies are told to be kind. Other lies are told to be mean. All lies, though, are in some way self-serving. Research by Dr. Bella DePaulo, who has studied deception for the last two decades, suggests that people lie most often about their feelings, actions, plans, and whereabouts. All lies also tend to be told for some sort of personal gain, for our own benefit. Could we really be that selfish in our lies? Yes, we could, and yes, we are. Even when we're lying in an attempt to benefit someone else— whether helping them, saving them from embarrassment, or sparing their feelings—there's generally something in it for us, too. We're somehow easing our own discomfort.

Scientists measure the movements of the earth, such as those generated by earthquakes and volcanic eruptions, with a seismometer, and they base the Richter magnitude scale on a logarithmic formula that assigns a single number—1 to 10—to represent the amount of energy released by an earthquake.

"Micro earthquakes," those that measure less than 2.0 on the Richter scale, are not felt. About eight thousand such earthquakes occur on our planet every day. Sliding up the scale, from 2.0 to 3.9, "minor earthquakes" may or may not be felt, but they are recorded and rarely cause damage. There are an estimated forty-nine thousand of these a year, and they are our most numerous type of earthquake.

"Light earthquakes," registering from 4.0 to 4.9, might cause a little shake, rattle, and roll but minimal damage.

A 5.0 "moderate quake" can cause moderate damage to poorly constructed buildings over small regions.

A 6.0 "strong" earthquake can be destructive in areas up to a hundred miles across in populated areas.

A 7.0 "major" earthquake can cause serious damage over broad areas and occurs an average of eighteen times a year on our planet.

An 8.0 "great" quake may occur once a year and causes serious damage in areas several hundred miles across. A 9.0 "great" quake can devastate an area thousands of miles across. Fortunately, one of these occurs only every twenty years or so.

A 10.0 earthquake has never been recorded.

As I write this chapter, the Japanese people are suffering from the devastating effects of an 8.9 magnitude earthquake off the coast of northeast Japan. The quake spawned a ferocious tsunami that caused massive destruction and thousands of deaths. It will take years, maybe several lifetimes, for the Japanese to recover.

It occurs to me that like earthquakes, our lies might have a similar scale of effect and damage. If we discuss lies as scientists do—evaluating the reasons for telling them and the damage done—there will be a hierarchy of lies that starts with the innocent, the fairly harmless, unnoticeable one, up to the 2.0 "little white lie." The lies will get more severe as we register higher on the scale, reaching toward the worst of lies—the magnitude 7.0s and higher—at the top of the Richter scale: lies that hurt, betray, and harm others.

Let's start small: the less than 2.0 lies that we tell thousands of times a day but aren't even noticed.

Many times in our daily lives we're asked, "How are you?" You're probably aware of this. "How are you?" has become more of a salutation than an actual question, but I found it an interesting exercise to count the number of times I was asked this question each day. I tracked several days this week. I logged 13 times on Friday; 20 times on Saturday, 11 of which occurred while shopping at the mall; and "How are you's" peaked at 32 on Tuesday when I taught school, worked at Fox, and went to the grocery store.

How do you answer this daily question? When I'm asked, I generally smile and say, "Fine, thanks." It's a stock response. As is the "How are you?" follow-up I habitually ask in return. Yet the truth is that some days I'm not fine. I'm tired. I'm over-worked. I'm feeling fat. My kids are driving me crazy. But does anyone except my very best friend or my mother really want (or need) to hear that?

Those who ask, "How are you doing?" generally do so as an act of communication, a "hello" between two acquaintances. More than a serious show of deep concern, this salutation is a tip of the hat to you, a conversation starter, an acknowledg-ment of an encounter. I have occasionally considered coming up with a clever response, a standard line such as, "If I were any better, I'd be twins," which I believe someone said to me once. Or perhaps I could pull off a snappy, "Feeling like myself!" Some executive trainers suggest that when asked, "How are you?" you should answer, "Great!" The belief is that if you say you're great enough times, you'll eventually believe it and *be* great.

I'll probably just stick with a simple "Fine. You?"

Registering a little higher on our "Richter scale of lying" are the day-to-day lies we tell that harm no one and sometimes might even help someone. These little "white lies" are occasion-ally felt and are sometimes considered to be a part of the greater good. Psychiatrist Dr. Dale Archer agrees. He told me, "If a white lie won't hurt, the average person doesn't have a problem telling that lie and never thinking about it again."

My Dani is a great little soccer player, but before we found soccer, she tried baseball, the sport her older brother, Jacob, excelled in. I'd go to game after game and watch as she'd miss every pitch (except once). During most games, she would just stand in the outfield looking at dandelions while the balls flew by. A few parents around me in the stands would yell out insults at their children for such infractions. More than once, I even heard (and ignored) a few directed at my own child. But could I tell my child she was never going to be the next Babe Ruth? No. Instead, I tried, "Way to watch that ball!" "Wonderful, Dani!" and "You go, girl!" just hoping to wake her up. When she ultimately decided that she hated baseball, instead of saying the very truthful, "I see why," I chose to focus on the positive: "Well, one thing's for sure, when you got that one hit, you really ran fast!" And that's how we found soccer.

I believe some Little League parents apparently come from the "radical honesty" school of thought. If you haven't been to a ball field recently, take my word for it—you'd blush to hear some of the things people yell at their kids, other people's kids, the coaches, and the referees. "Idiot!" "That's crummy!" And "You suck!" were all things I heard while sitting on the stands surrounded by "adults." It became so brutally honest (also known as "viciously mean") that in order to protect the kids, the "silent game" was instituted. No sounds could come from the crowd, except applause. We could clap until our hands were raw, but not one peep was allowed to come out of our mouths. The penalty for an infraction? The rule breaker would be escorted out. I watched a few parents get dragged out, including one very unhappy grandma. The "silent game" made for some very peaceful games and little ball player egos that weren't bruised as we rode home. The silent game, like a little white lie, often kept spirits from getting squelched.

Sometimes in day-to-day life, we tell little white lies for our personal benefit. These graph a little higher on our Richter scale, not for the damage they do to others, but for the damage they do to us personally.

I have told people more than once, "I got it on sale," because I didn't want to admit I'd paid full price. And I've gotten out of a work assignment by saying my kid wasn't feeling well. I know I need to rethink these little white lies. Do I just use these small tales as a way to prevent my own discomfort? Couldn't I, for example, simply say that I overpaid or put something on my credit card that I know I shouldn't have? Yes. Couldn't I just tell my boss that I am exhausted and need a day to catch my breath? Absolutely. Yes, I realize I probably should tell the truth on these occasions. As proof, I told both of these white lies months ago, and I'm still thinking about them. I have unhealthy guilt.

---

### TRUTH ADVANTAGE DO'S AND DON'TS!

If you have to deliver a message that's negative, **DO** find something to point out that's positive.

**DON'T** use honesty passive-aggressively as a sword to cut into someone's self-esteem.

---

Lies that venture into 5.0 territory are those that are told for what St. Augustine called "the pleasure of lying." Rather than telling a tale simply to protect themselves from the consequences of being honest, there's another type of lie: when people state an outright inaccuracy without feeling any associated guilt. Lying for lying's sake. In your day, you've probably encountered one or two people who tell lies this way. A person like this just can't help himself. He loves to lie, and he lies about everything: His salary. His heredity. His ailments. Other people, places, and things. Any occasion is a fine occasion to lie.

Let's face it, this person has an illness. Although he may not tell his lies to harm you, it's hard to maintain a sincere friendship with someone who is not truthful.

My now thirteen-year-old daughter, Dani, and I were recently having a serious discussion. I had noticed that she was no longer talking to a close friend of hers or even mentioning the girl's name, so one morning I asked her why. "She lies," Dani said matter-of-factly, as she ate her bowl of cereal. "And I can't trust her anymore." I asked her whether the lie was so bad that she had to end the friendship. "Look, Mom," my daughter said emphatically. "I know when someone is a liar, and she lied for a long time, and it was hurting people. I don't want to be friends with her. It's as simple as that." She went back to eating her cereal, but the brief conversation was a lesson for me. My daughter was old enough to make a judgment call about character, and I, too, could probably use a bit of her certitude when dealing with people who lie. I tend to give people the benefit of the doubt one too many times. Dani had a simple point. Why should we waste time on liars? Move on!

Had Dani not been so resolute, I would have carried on the conversation a little further to figure out the severity of the lies told by this young girl. Was she saying her dad is an astronaut, when he's in fact a car salesman? Or was it more serious? For example, saying malicious things about other friends at school? Or worse, about my sweet Dani! Whatever it was, it so bothered Dani that she decided to call the friendship quits. And, as her mother, I decided to accept that.

"The best way to determine whether to trust someone evolves over time, over experience," Dr. Dale Archer told me. "We learn to trust over the long term, and a variety of incidents that come up in a relationship will let you know whether you can trust someone or not. We lose trust when a person says one thing and does another." So, Dani might be on to something.

Charting the highest on our Richter scale of lies are serious lies. These are lies that hurt, harm, or betray others and range from damaging to completely destructive. When these whoppers hit, they don't merely break the dishes; instead, the earth cracks beneath us, and the whole house falls in.

"One should rather die than be betrayed," Steven Deitz said. "There is no deceit in death. It delivers precisely what it has promised. Betrayal, though . . . betrayal is the willful slaughter of hope."

My kids and I were sitting around the dinner table one night, when I asked them what they felt was the worst thing a friend could do to another friend. Jacob immediately said, "Talk behind your back," and Dani said, "Diss you!" Yes, dissing someone is very middle school, but both of my children said that a friend lying about you is the worst thing one friend can do to another. The Ten Commandments come to mind: "Though shalt not bear false witness against your neighbor."

# Gossip

There's an old Irish saying that says, "Who gossips with you will gossip about you."

When I was a prosecutor, Julie (another prosecutor) often stopped by my office and plopped into my guest chair. She started the conversation by asking about my cases, what I was working on, and what my theories on some of my cases were. She was, at first, very business oriented. Then she usually asked, "How's your son? What are your plans for the weekend?" Yet all of that was only the buildup for her real intent, as she worked up to some big office rumor:. . . "Did you hear that Colleen's husband is cheating on her? I'm not sure Colleen even knows. Can you believe that?"

Now, if Julie were known in the office to be an honest person, I probably would have engaged in the conversation, with the intention of figuring out whether I could do something for Colleen's well-being and happiness. But Julie had a reputation as the office nosy parker, trading on rumors that she herself would start in order to pry information out of the person she was "informing" of her news. Knowing that, I always responded coolly with something like, "Oh, that's too bad. I've got to get back to work." Julie then made her way down the hall a few offices and started all over again with the next person. She became an office bad joke.

Like the boy who cried wolf, no one believed a thing Julie said.

The saddest part of the "joke" was that if we wanted to spread something around the office, we all knew simply to tell Julie. Worse, I always worried that if Julie could fabricate rumors about her office pals, in what other areas was she capable of fabricating information? Evidence in a criminal case? I never saw any proof of that, but the rumormonger aspect of her personality made me suspicious of all of her actions.

There's a difference between gossip and rumor. Gossip is talking with other people about other people.

We are hard-wired to be attracted to it, and researchers are finding that it is a natural part of social bonding. In the past, gossip was a survival tool in which small groups of people passed along important news about other groups of people. A rumor is pure conjecture: passing along something that we don't know is true, almost like a fishing expedition. Rumors bear false witness.

The question we each need to ask ourselves is this: Do I want to give my friends and colleagues any reason to doubt what I say?

## We Lie to Get Attention

Sometimes we concoct lies to bring ourselves glory, but these fabrications also adversely affect the lives of others. I'm reminded of Debbie Swenson, a forty-year-old Kansas woman, who created a blog about her daughter Kaycee's fight with cancer. Unfortunately, the sad truth was that Debbie was lying. She had invented a daughter and given the girl an illness in order to attract attention to herself. She used a neighbor's photos and posted stories, as Kaycee, of her heartbreaking struggle. Kaycee's plight garnered much attention on the Internet and earned her thousands of friends.

When Kaycee "died," her friends were devastated; many wanted to attend her funeral. That's when the hard truth was discovered: Debbie had made it all up. The thousands of people who had read her diary, followed her story, and prayed for her were rightly upset. How could a person lie about something so serious? Debbie defended herself by saying that Kaycee was a loving combination of all of the cancer victims she'd known. Because Debbie had never asked for money, she could not be charged with a crime.

Yet the real crime here was her lack of authenticity. No one wants a friend who isn't real. Before you create a phony story to make yourself look better, you might realize that when the real truth is discovered, you'll look worse.

## We Lie to Get out of Something

I've already discussed a little fudging to get out of work or a dinner date, but there are far more serious lies that hurt others, often those we love most. *Parade Magazine* polled Americans and asked, "Have you ever lied to your spouse about the cost of something you bought?" In response, 72 percent said yes, and 28 percent said no. But that's just the tip of the iceberg. I know of a woman I'll call Dana. She had run up a huge debt on her credit card and couldn't pay. She was getting badgered and threatened by collection agencies and was afraid her husband would find out.

What did she do? Rather than facing her circumstances and 'fessing up, she made it worse. Unbeknownst to her husband, she secretly dipped into the line of credit on their home. Her husband learned of Dana's lies when he received a Notice of Default by certified mail. Their marriage survived, but their house didn't.

Financially is not the only way that we may end up hurting, harming, or betraying a person when we lie to get out of something. Do you remember the story of Jennifer Wilbanks, the Georgia bride-to-be who disappeared for three days in 2005, while the police and her family anxiously searched for her, fearing for her safety and dreading the worst? When she was finally found in New Mexico, she told police that she had been kidnapped and sexually assaulted. She described in specific detail her kidnappers: "a Hispanic male with short black hair and rotten teeth and a heavy-set white female with blonde, frosted, shoulder-length hair."

When the police began to question her story, Wilbanks confessed that she had made the whole thing up. It was all a lie. She merely had cold feet about her wedding and wanted to get away for a few days to clear her head. She was charged with giving false information to the police but received only two years' probation and 120 hours of community service. What she did to her family and her fiancé was extraordinarily hurtful. Needless to say, the wedding was called off.

Lying to get out of something only gets you into a worse situation. Before you concoct a crazy lie to circumvent facing a truth, realize that it will cause much less pain in the long term simply to be honest. Rip the Band-Aid off, don't try to cover it up with a bigger one.

## We Lie to Steal

Betrayal can take on many forms. A wedding photographer for my friend's wedding ran off with half of her down payment but, even worse, skipped town on the day of the wedding.

When, after numerous calls, she finally figured out that he wasn't going to show, she burst into tears. The stolen money was one thing, but the photographer had stolen her keepsake memories and a whole lot of joy, too.

Remember Enron? At one time, Enron was the largest energy trader in the world. The year after it reported revenues of $101 billion, it collapsed in only twenty-four days, leaving twenty-two thousand employees jobless. Many found their entire life savings wiped out because their 401(k)s had been frozen. Leaders Kenneth Lay and Jeffrey Skilling had intentionally lied about the health of the company, while surreptitiously dumping a half billion dollars' worth of their own stock. Enron declared bankruptcy in December 2001—after its stock slid from $90 a share to less than $1 a share in a matter of weeks.

The Enron scandal has been described as the corporate crime of the previous century, and it forced an overhaul of U.S financial regulations. All of the firm's success was built on lies—from shady accounting to a gross understatement of the company's debt and overestimation of its profits. Unlike the situations described previously, in which people backed themselves into a corner and lied to get out of the mess they had created, the Enron masterminds—Lay and Skilling—deliberately misled, lied to, and hurt others without having any moral qualms. It was all about the money. They lied purely out of greed.

Once he was caught, Bernie Madoff, another lying crook you may have heard of, admitted that his investment firm was "just one big lie." Madoff used a "Ponzi scheme" for more than a decade to keep bilking his investors for billions. Named after Charles Ponzi, a notorious schemer from the early twentieth century, a Ponzi scheme is a lie built on a lie—a traitor takes money from an investor, and, rather than investing it, he keeps some for himself and uses some to pay off earlier investors.

What was shocking about Madoff's scheme was that he had once been the chairman of NASDAQ and had been a respected, successful expert in the financial field. Yet like many people, he became consumed by greed, and his lies allowed him to walk away with billions of dollars. In 2008, Madoff confessed to conning $50 billion from unsuspecting investors who entrusted him with their money.

These stories of lies for financial gain unfolded with the wallop of a Greek tragedy. In 2004, Ken Lay was convicted and died while awaiting sentencing. In 2006, Jeffrey Skilling was convicted of multiple federal felony charges, and he is currently behind bars, thinking about his lies as he serves a twenty-four-year prison sentence. Yet his lies did the most damage to those closest to him. In February 2011, Skilling's twenty-year-old son was found dead, lying near bottles of medication.

In March 2009, Bernie Madoff pleaded guilty to eleven federal felonies of defrauding thousands of investors of billions of dollars. He was sentenced to 150 years in prison, the maximum allowed sentence. Like Skilling and others who commit such betrayals, Madoff's family was hit by more tragedy. His guilty plea and imprisonment did not stop the ripple effect. On the morning of December 11, 2010—exactly two years after Bernard's arrest—his elder son, Mark Madoff, age forty-six, was found dead in his New York City apartment, hanging by a black dog leash. His two-year-old son, Nicholas, was sleeping in a nearby bedroom, as was Grouper, their Labradoodle. Around 4 a.m., he had sent three wrenching e-mails. He wrote to his lawyer, "No one wants to hear the truth. Take care of my family." And to his wife, who was vacationing at Disney World, he said, "I love you. Send someone to take care of Nick."

## We Lie out of Selfishness to Protect the Self

Research suggests that we lie most often to those we love because we care about what they think of us. We want to be loved.

If you've ever known people who found out their partners were cheating on them, you know it is a lie with long-term emotional consequences. Often the partner who discovers such a horrible truth feels somehow responsible for the transgression and suffers a grave sense of shame. Yet it is earth shattering not only to the unsuspecting spouse, but also to the lives of the children. Even if they aren't aware of the specifics, they sense the change in dynamics and often feel that their worlds have suddenly been turned upside down. The breech in trust is almost irreparable.

Consider the harm caused by Tiger Woods's transgressions, not only to himself and his career, but to his family as well. Forget the million-dollar endorsement deals and the sponsors that dropped him like a hot potato—the wealthiest athlete on the planet hurt the lives of his wife, his children, his mother, and his business partners. As mistress after mistress came forward to tell her story of bedding Tiger, I couldn't help but think that each new revelation must have been death by a thousand paper cuts for his wife, Elin.

The cost of Tiger's infidelity is enormous. Not only did he fall from high public regard, but his wife divorced him, and his children now live in Sweden. Furthermore, his mother, who reportedly had to deal with infidelities in her own marriage, was said to be hurt, angry, and disappointed by his behavior. A friend told *People* magazine that she "wants to know how he could do this to his family."

Tiger released a statement about his mistake:

"I am deeply aware of the disappointment and hurt that my infidelity has caused to so many people, most of all my wife and children. I want to say again to everyone that I am profoundly sorry and that I ask forgiveness. It may not be possible to repair the damage I've done, but I want to do my best to try.

"I would like to ask everyone, including my fans, the good people at my foundation, business partners, the PGA Tour, and my fellow competitors, for their understanding. What's most important now is that my family has the time, privacy, and safe haven we will need for personal healing.

"After much soul searching, I have decided to take an indefinite break from professional golf. I need to focus my attention on being a better husband, father, and person.

"Again, I ask for privacy for my family and I am especially grateful for all those who have offered compassion and concern during this difficult period."

Well, as we know, it didn't turn out so well. He's back but not winning in golf, divorced, and thousands of miles from his children, and he has lost hundreds of millions of dollars. What truly worries me about lies of this magnitude are not only the pain in the short term or the financial loss, but the emotional price that the lie will extract for years to come. Elin has to forever endure the nightmarish glare of the spotlight, but just consider how his children may be affected as they grow up and learn how badly their father behaved.

I am sure the soul searching might be "indefinite." No matter how Tiger apologizes or how many millions Elin gained from their divorce settlement, nothing can ever compensate for the pain and suffering he caused his family. As William E. Gladstone put it, "Selfishness is the greatest curse of the human race."

Know that lies of this nature will destroy not only your life, but the lives of those you love.

## We Lie Because We're Evil

Measuring a clear 10.0 on our Richter scale of lying would be lies against humanity. The lies and deceptions of someone like Adolf Hitler. Knowing that you are not that person, I will say, Be thankful you are you and that you use the truth to become the best person possible.

"The worst lies are the lies we tell ourselves," said Richard Bach, the writer of the great fable *Jonathan Livingston Seagull*, which chronicles a seagull learning about life and self-protection. "We live in denial of what we do, even what we think. We do this because we're afraid. We fear we will not find love, and when we find it we fear we'll lose it. We fear that if we do not have love we will be unhappy."

Humans will continue to find reasons to lie. Even the most honest person you know probably lies from time to time: "Your dinner was delicious." "Your hair looks great." "Your baby is beautiful." These minor quakes can be forgiven, but for real relationships to survive and prosper, there is no place for anything but truth.

Dr. Mark L. Knapp gave me a quick way to assess whether I should say something that is even the slightest bit untrue. "Will you admit and be accountable for your lie?" he asked. "How will you defend it? For some lies, the consequences of discovery will be minimal, but liars often put such issues out of their minds. As a result, liars often imagine 'things will work out okay,' even with lies that have huge consequences. The 'bigger' the lie (the greater impact, the more important the issue, the more reprehensible the lie, the more people involved, etc.) the more the liar has at stake and the more work he or she will put into keeping the lie from being discovered. But we also know that 'big' lies are often detected. This may be a result of the correspondingly greater desire to detect 'big' lies, the greater guilt experienced by the teller, or both."

I have heard it said that "character is what happens behind closed doors when no one is looking" and that a person of good character doesn't lie. I'll simply ask you this, *Who do you want to be when you are alone with yourself, with your thoughts, with your actions and deeds? Why do anything to weigh yourself down or not be proud of?* Here is life's challenge: Put the pedal to your mettle and become a person who is known for your integrity, your honor, and your trust.

The truth will be your advantage. In part 2, you will see how to claim it, use it, become it.

The next chapter, "The Lie Detector," will help you figure out whether someone is not being truthful with you.

---

## THE TRUTH ADVANTAGE CHECKUP
### *"Of course, I love your brussels sprouts!"*

**We're all a bunch of liars.**
- Realize that most of us lie about all sorts of things, from the smallest, such as liking a friend's cooking, to the biggest, such as covering up an affair.
- If you just said, "Not me," think again.
- Note that you might be surprised if you write down every white lie you tell in one day.

**Little lies bother people, too.**
- Realize that just because you haven't covered up an affair or taken credit for a coworker's project doesn't mean the little lies you tell are acceptable.
- Note that people are often bothered by little lies because they think it indicates that someone is prone to more untruthfulness.
- Know that if you fib a little, people don't trust you a lot.

**I care about me, me, and . . . oh, me.**
- Realize that we lie because we think we're protecting ourselves.
- Know that lying has consequences for the people we care about the most.
- Think about what your lies might cost you before you utter them.

---

# CHAPTER 5

# The Lie Detector

*Liars need good memories.*

—FRENCH PROVERB

W hen dealing with people in everyday life, wouldn't it be great if you had a portable lie detector? You wouldn't have to wonder whether your friend was actually busy Thursday night or just flaking out on your plans, why your date never called you a second time, or whether your husband really does have to stay late at the office. You'd also find out how much your boss is paying the rest of the office workers and exactly what the dealer will accept as the lowest price on the new car you want.

Daniel Craven, the creator of HonestParenting.com, told me, "Becoming proficient at knowing when someone is lying would be a worthwhile skill in personal life, as well as in legal and governmental arenas, whether it's an exact science or not. Of course, it might also cause a few divorces!"

I know that as a parent, I'd love to have my very own personal, portable lie detector at the ready. The adage "You're not your kids' friend, you're their parent" is so true. I will admit to snooping through my children's diaries, monitoring their Facebook accounts, and even cross-examining them at times. For example, when my daughter was turning six (yes, six), I had a big birthday party planned for her and a beautiful cake. Yet when I went to get the cake from the study where I'd hidden it, the whole thing had been destroyed. Where there had been frosting, there were now big bald spots. The frosting had been licked off! In a panic, I ran to a local bakery and asked whether they could fix it for me in a hurry. There was no time for homemade icing. They saw a mom in a panic and kindly fixed the cake.

After I got home, I used my courtroom cross-examination skills to get the truth out of my daughter. The conversation was as simple as this:

Me: Did you touch your birthday cake?
Daughter: No.
Me: Not even for a second?
Daughter: No.
Me: Good. But I'm a little worried you won't like the icing.
Daughter: No, I like it.

This worked when Dani was six years old, but it gets harder as she becomes older and wiser to my ways.

Galileo Galilei said, "All truths are easy to understand once they are discovered; the point is to discover them." How do you discover them, though? How do you tell whether someone is being truthful with you? What are the indicators that a person is hiding something? And what is the best way to handle the situation when you do sense an individual's dishonesty? In the second part of the book, I'll set forth the seven keys to becoming more truthful in your life. First, however, I should give you a little guidance on how to see, and protect yourself from, other people's deception.

Since the beginning of time, even before the invention of words, we've been searching for the truth and for methods of getting the truth out of others. We have invented torture devices and interrogation techniques and have measured brain waves, heartbeat, breath rate, and any other thing that moves in order to determine the truth. Yet polygraphs are still not admissible evidence in court, because they aren't scientifically reliable enough. Any old sociopath can beat a lie detector test. "Some people are good liars," Dr. Dale Archer said, explaining the difficulty of detection. "Sometimes you can sense it, sometimes not. If we always could tell whether someone was lying, poker wouldn't be a popular game, but it is!"

In *Meet the Parents*, Ben Stiller goes to meet Robert DeNiro, his future father-in-law, who also happens to be a retired CIA operative. It's impossible not to laugh when Stiller is coerced into an impromptu at-home lie detector test and asked such questions as "Are you going to cheat on my daughter?" and "Have you ever purchased pornographic material?" Stiller nervously sweats it out.

I know the feeling. I couldn't get away with anything living in a house with my own FBI agent father. But not everyone has a father who is an FBI agent or has a portable lie detector in the house. (Nor would most people want one!) And not every lie is as seemingly obvious as a receipt for flowers and lipstick on the collar. So what can you do to recognize and cut through mistruths and get people to work with you to cultivate mutual trust and respect?

As a prosecutor, I couldn't go into the courtroom unless I absolutely believed in the case. Ethically, I couldn't even bring a case unless I really believed that I had the truth on my side. I always had to get to the truth. I learned in dealing with criminals that there is nothing as obvious as Pinocchio's nose, but there are definitive ways to ascertain whether someone is telling you the truth, namely:

1. Listening for *verbal cues*;
2. Looking for *physical cues*; and
3. Studying the *forensics* (that is, the trail of evidence people often leave behind when they're not telling the truth).

Your friends, colleagues, and family aren't criminals, though, so how can you discover the truth from them, kindly and respectfully, without making them suspicious or angry or feel as if they are sitting on the witness stand?

Here are the secrets to becoming your very own lie detector.

## Verbal Clues

What does a lie sound like? If lies are complex, people might speak more slowly and pause more often, and if lies are simple or have been well rehearsed, the speaker might be perfectly fluent in fibbing. I know from standing in front of a jury that a liar's testimony is often more persuasive to jurors than a truth teller's testimony because liars generally tell a story with the events in chronological order. Honest people often present their version of what happened in an improvised jumble.

> Truth teller: "I went into the gas station and bought a pack of gum."
> Question: "Oh, did you use a charge card or pay cash?"
> Truth teller: "Cash. I stopped at the ATM before I went to the gas station."

A liar will say, "I remember the night very clearly. I was driving down the road. I noticed a full moon. I went to the ATM.

I got a hundred dollars, four twenties and two tens. Then I pulled up to the gas station, went inside, and bought a pack of spearmint gum." In addition to the very clear sequence of events, he also delivered his story without any hesitation words—no "um" or "er"—and no pauses. An unsuspecting jury (and you, the believer) will think he's a brilliant speaker with a great memory. Why? He told his story so well! He doesn't have a brilliant memory; his story has been thought through and rehearsed. Once you start to notice these patterns, you'll be able to spot when someone is speaking unnaturally well.

In a typical conversation with your friend, isn't it natural for you to occasionally ask for points of clarification? Your friend might say, "After the gym, I had to pick the kids up from ball practice, and, um, then go to a meeting at the school straight from there." And you ask, "You went to a school meeting in your gym clothes?" "Oh," she says, "I forgot I stopped at the house for a quick change!"

When I questioned people accused of a crime, I frequently discovered that those who were lying often sounded as if they were reading from a script. They told their stories in such a convincing way because they desperately wanted them to sound true. They didn't stumble or correct themselves as we all do in daily conversations because they figured that this would be a red flag that they were trying to deceive people. I think it's exactly the opposite.

I have found that if someone is overprepared or has every minute detail in his or her story accounted for, there's reason for doubt or at least for further questions. There are also "tells"—words to listen for in conversation, such as *never* and *always*—that indicate someone may not be giving you the whole truth and nothing but the truth. I call these "lie alarms." As a prosecutor, I usually cringed whenever a police officer said that he "always" checks the backseat before getting in the car or when a witness went into such specific detail about what someone was wearing six months ago or exactly how far away something was. I knew that the jurors would realize, as I did, that it's not often that we "always" do something, nor are we able to remember minutiae from months ago and calculate that the distance across the room is 15½ feet. I can hardly remember specifically what I ate for breakfast or wore yesterday!

A study conducted at Stanford's Graduate School of Business analyzed the transcripts of nearly thirty thousand conference calls between 2003 and 2007 made by American CEOs. The researchers were later able to analyze each company's profits and corporate success, as compared to what these executives had said about their firms' financial status. The study found that deceptive bosses avoid the word *I* and instead talk a lot about *we*, and they use more general knowledge references, such as "as you know," than they do references to specific points about shareholder value or minimizing the risk of a lawsuit. They also use fewer "non-extreme positive emotion words." So, instead of calling something "good," the deceptive executive would call it "fantastic."

William Daly, a former FBI investigator and now an executive with a leading international security investigations firm, told me that he looks for contractions when a person is answering his questions. Words such as *doesn't*, *couldn't*, and *wasn't* are more likely to be used by a person telling the truth. A liar would attempt to be more precise and would probably say *does not*, *could not*, and *was not*.

In questioning witnesses, I always noted when someone repeated my question. It was typically a person telling a lie. For example,

Q: Do you know why someone would want to kill your wife?
A: Do I know why someone would want to kill my wife?

The only reason to repeat the question is to give yourself time to think. Most people, certainly honest ones, would immediately scream, "No!"

I was also quick to note when someone answered a question with "Swear on my mother's grave" or "As God is my witness" or the like. It always seemed to me a little like "The lady doth protest too much, methinks." Similarly, when people told me to "ask anyone how honest I am" or suggested that I check with their preacher, teacher, brother, or mother, to vouch for their honesty, I always found it a little fishy.

Another of my lie alarms is hearing someone's voice crack or change pitch during his or her delivery. Unless we're dealing with a teenage boy, pitch inconsistencies and vocal hiccups are often a sign that nerves are on edge or breath patterns have changed.

Yet words only scratch the surface. It's what's under and behind those words that often tells you what you need to know.

# Physical Clues

We're wired to believe people, predisposed to take what people tell us as the truth. (I think that's a good thing. We should believe first, doubt second. Innocent until proven guilty.) We believe people because they "look" believable, because they "act" believable, and because they "seem" believable.

Yet further inspection can be enlightening. Physical clues can lead us to the truth. We humans have a "fight or flight" response. When we're questioned about our wrongdoing, we want to run, and if we can't, we fidget, we wiggle, and we twitch. When people aren't telling the truth, their bodies become billboards that scream, "You're right. I'm wrong. I'm lying to you!"

As we've seen, not being truthful with others causes us discomfort. It manifests in a physical way. Jury consultants who help select honest jurors report that shrugging or excessive blinking can tip off the careful observer about a lie in progress. Have you ever noticed that children wring their hands or touch their heads when they are not being truthful? Watch your children closely, you'll see it.

Let's talk about eyes. When I first moved to New York, everyone told me, "don't look anyone in the eye" as a safety precaution. But I think not looking someone in the eye is telling. Remember, the old expression your mom probably said to you at least once: "Look me straight in the eye and say that?" If you couldn't look her in the eye, she knew you weren't telling the truth. Eyes are a pretty good indicator of honesty. If you can't look someone in the eye, it's a signal that something is not quite right. Either you're trying to protect yourself or there's a high probability there's a lie flying around. It's a classic giveaway. Even kids on the playground know this. In fact, a 2008 study reported by the American Psychological Association found that children recognize that a speaker's shifty eyes might indicate lying. Sensitivity to gaze is something we learn early on, and that tendency to perceive gaze aversion as a lying cue continues through adulthood.

Jury consultants taught me that when people look to the right, that indicates a creative process. So, if you're asking someone a tough question and his eyes dart rightward, it might indicate that he is making something up. If his eyes look to the left, it generally indicates the mind is searching for a fact. Test this theory out on someone by asking both a creative question and a factual question. For example, "Give me a weird animal sound" would be a creative question. Your subject would most likely glance to the right in order to think it through. If you ask, "What was the first song you ever learned?" the subject's eyes will probably dart leftward to think about or try to remember the fact.

Nothing is a bigger signal than what is said with your eyes— the windows to your soul—but body language experts point out that other physical body cues might also indicate deception. According to Tonya Reiman, a leading body language expert, in order to understand someone's nonverbal signals and tell whether the person is lying, you must first understand what his or her normal behavior is. You must first figure out the individual's "baseline" behavior. Put simply, a truth signal is the way someone speaks, acts, and gestures under normal conditions and not when he or she is under pressure. This "norming" works on the same principle as an actual polygraph machine.

"Your goal is to notice someone else's signals when he is calm," Reiman explained to me. "How is his handshake—dominant, neutral, or submissive? How is the person standing? What is the position of his trunk and torso? Does he orient toward or away from you? What type of gestures does he use— high upper gestures or lower gestures? What is his neutral facial expression? What about his eyes? Does he maintain eye contact while he speaks, and how often does he seem to blink? In addition, what is his normal eye position when speaking and remembering? Watch where the eyes go as he answers. Does he look up left or right, side left or right, or down left or right? What is the norm for the individual's eye contact? When he is lying, there is a good chance you will note a deviation from that norm."

Once someone is hooked up to a lie detector, the polygrapher asks a few straightforward, fact-based questions. As a human lie detector, you will surely use this technique as well; it's the same one that lawyers use when questioning a witness in court.

Q: "Is your name Colonel Mustard?"
A: "Yes."
Q: "What color are you?"
A: "I'm the yellow figurine."

Q: "And where do you live, sir?"
A: "I'm from Yellow Square."

Now we have our baseline read on his physical signals, and we gain an understanding of how he acts under normal questioning. Then, you, the polygrapher, will ask the question that you suspect will provoke an untruthful answer:

Q: "Did you kill Mr. Boddy in the conservatory?"
A: "No!"
Q: "Have you, sir, ever held a candlestick?"
A: "No!"

The difference between the colonel's voice and physicality when asked a mundane question, as opposed to the provocative question, begins to tell the true story.

Everything an individual does reveals something, from the handshake to the voice, from the way someone stands to the way he or she sits. With your friends and loved ones, you generally know the norm. When they stray from that norm, grow anxious, or have a change in behavior, you can bet something is up.

Research has suggested that between 60 and 70 percent of the meaning in conversation is derived from nonverbal behavior. Body language, from gestures to eye movements, speaks volumes. We all give and receive such signals unconsciously. Communications expert Matthew McKay, for instance, suggests that hands on your knees indicates readiness, hands on your hips reveals impatience, and hands behind your back suggests self-control.

William Daly, a former FBI investigator, said that the FBI technique is to notice the little things. "For the investigator," he said, "the myriad of subtleties may be referred to as a person's demeanor. If I were to characterize a couple of nonverbal signals that someone may be lying, I would say the uncontrolled eye movement away from the interviewer (down, up, sideways).

An additional nonverbal sign that I have found indicative of someone lying is when they rub their hands over their mouths or perhaps talking into the hand that is hovering over the mouth."

What I found in questioning witnesses, victims, and criminals is that often liars do not use their hands. If they do, they touch or cover their mouths. They also might touch their noses. In fact, there's a term for this. It's called the *Pinocchio effect*. In addition, they might physically try to put something between themselves and you to take a little of the pressure off, from a coffee cup to a pocketbook. It subconsciously provides them with a wall or a shield.

A jury consultant once told me that people think they can hide a lie behind a smile, but, properly noted, the expressions that flash on a face are like billboards that display what someone is really thinking and saying. There are laugh lines, and there are "lie" lines. The human face has nearly ninety muscles that can combine into more than ten thousand facial configurations, about half of which, from furrowed brows to raised eyebrows, can give us an indication of the truth of what someone is saying or the subtext of what a person is thinking. Watch carefully. If someone says, "I'm so sorry to hear that!" and then has a delayed sad expression, he or she might be deceiving you. Yet a genuine person's words and sentiment match like a great outfit.

Tonya Reiman says that once you've "baselined" someone (know the person's "normal"), there are indeed physical signals that she considers red flags for deception. These are the little things to look for.

### The Physical Language of Liars

- Increased blink rate
- Change in the person's visual access cues
- Pupil dilation

- Avoiding, or the overuse of, eye contact
- Looking down and away after speaking
- Hand to head, including:
  - Eye rubbing, itching, or the pretense of having something in the eye
  - Scratching
  - Touching the nose
  - Rubbing the ear
  - Covering the mouth
- Tongue protrusion/lip lick
- Increased swallowing
- Reddening/blushing/perspiration, including moisture above the lip or the brow
- Use of the nondominant hand for emphasis
- Indignant finger point
- Using a barrier, such as a bag or a cup
- Hiding the hands
- Fidgety digits and/or movements
- Shoulder and palm shrugs when saying yes
- Decrease in body movement or nonverbal lockdown
- Facing and angling away
- The timing of gestures is off

It's a whole body thing—tapping toes, fidgety fingers, profuse sweating, or a dry mouth. How can we forget Bill Clinton's wagging finger, "I did not have sexual relations with that woman." Women specifically tend to lick their lips, hide their hands, and exhibit changes in skin tone when lying.

Although there is no one absolute "tell" (verbal or nonverbal) to prove someone is lying, people certainly give off signals that indicate they are experiencing heightened anxiety or arousal when compared to their typical behavior. But we need more, right?

That's where forensics comes into play.

# Forensics

We all know the old adage "Don't judge a book by its cover." Well, that's never truer than when you're trying to get to the truth. I learned from criminals that a good liar can charm, convince, and win you over with a genuine smile. Why? Because they are good liars and can look "normal" or better than normal. Many times, the real criminal is not the incoherent person you hear babbling on the street. No, it's the nice guy or gal at the sales counter, your tough but fair gym instructor, or the guy in the next cubicle who seems so nice.

As a federal prosecutor, I was trained to sniff out the bad guys. My specialty was murder-for-hire. It wasn't a title that fit easily on my federal business card, but the cases fascinated me. What would lead a seemingly rational person to choose such a dire end for another person, usually someone the individual was supposed to love? Money must be the motive, I assumed. Yet I found that although money was always a factor, it wasn't ever the primary motivator. Money wasn't what drove them to it.

Power, saving face, and "having it all" were much stronger drives. Take the case of the upstanding Boeing engineer I prosecuted who chose the "hiring" route when faced with divorce. He told his hired hit man that he had a "five-foot-four-inch" problem in need of taking care of." For him, the shame of his wife divorcing him was simply intolerable. (Fortunately for her, the hit man was an undercover FBI agent.)

As a reporter and an analyst, I've covered some of the worst murder cases. Again, money wasn't the sole motivating factor, and the criminal could talk a good game. Good looks and status in society were no predictors of honesty. Just think of Scott Peterson, the handsome fertilizer salesman from Modesto, California, married to his beautiful wife, Laci, and baby already named "Conner" on the way. I covered that case from preliminary hearing to sentencing. At the sentencing, I'll never forget the chilling words of Laci's mother, Sharon Rocha, when she exclaimed, "You, Scott, are proof that evil can lurk anywhere. You don't have to look evil to be evil. The logical solution would be divorce." For Peterson, divorce would have meant loss of face and loss of power—he simply wouldn't be getting his way.

Watching Peterson day after day in the courtroom stare blankly ahead, and listening to all of the lies he'd told along the way, I marveled at what good liars some people are. As Dr. Dale Archer, the renowned psychiatrist, explained, "The best liars have no regard for the rules of society. They lie without remorse, that's why they are so good at it." Dr. Archer told me, "Train yourself to feel, not just to be logical. Trust that gut feeling. It could save your life."

In the courtroom, I always told my witnesses and investigators that there were twenty-four eyes on everything they did. Those twelve jurors were watching every detail, every action, and every response. At the end of the day, those twenty-four eyeballs would determine who was lying and who was telling the truth.

Now I'm no longer a prosecutor but a mother of two teenagers, and, like all mothers, I worry for my children. I worry about the people they meet and the lies they'll be told. Using my training as a prosecutor and a reporter, I've tried to school my children in ways to protect themselves and to keep an eye out for something amiss.

Yes, you can listen to what someone says, you can look at his body language, but in the end, it's proof that will finally convince you. How do you get proof?

Doing wrong isn't always something people think through before they do it. So, when the deed is done, they wonder, "Uh oh, how am I going to get out of this?" And a lie is born. A liar always makes a mistake, always leaves something behind. Prisons prove that. We all leave a trail of evidence showing where we've been and what we've done, leaving our "finger-print" of having been there, done that.

It's just a matter of digging for the mistake.

---

TRUTH ADVANTAGE DO'S AND DON'TS!

DO trust your gut . . . if something looks or sounds off, it probably is.

DON'T become the cynical, suspicious person who assumes everyone is out to get you.

---

Forensics refers to the trail of evidence that liars often leave behind—the cheating girlfriend's most recent credit card bill showing a charge for a motel room with heart-shaped beds and an hourly rate or her text message log reflecting a list of sugges-tive texts to her good-looking boss. Such evidence can also include the nature of the conversations someone has with you when he or she is trying to cover something up. If you're attempt-ing to find out whether that same beloved girlfriend is cheating, for example, and you ask, "Where were you?" it's easy for her to answer, "Dinner." Yet as questions become more specific, they become more difficult for the lying person to answer. Asking for details is often a way to catch a lie. "What restaurant?" "What'd you eat?" The initial lie is easy, the subsequent ones grow harder and harder to cover up. "Um, Guido's Italian Restaurant." "Eh . . . Caesar . . . I mean, Caesar's salad?"

Let me give you an example of a situation where only one question was needed to get to the truth. I heard the story of four local high school boys who decided that a gorgeous spring day was the perfect time to cut class. When they showed up at school after lunch, they told their teacher they'd had a flat tire. They were relieved when she smiled and said, "No problem, but you missed a quiz this morning, so take out a sheet of paper and grab a seat away from each other." She waited for them to sit down and said, "Just one question: which tire was flat?"

The goal of any lie detector, any interrogation, or any question is to get to the truth. The route to the truth is to look for inconsistencies or gaps that move the subject away from the person's initial statements and start to erode his or her story.

Former FBI investigator William Daly told me, "I think that most people want to believe that others are being honest with them, whether it is in personal or business matters. People want people to be honest with them so their default mechanism is set to 'I want to believe you.' People haven't honed their sensors to tell if people are lying. I think people can learn or change in this regard, but it takes two things: (1) they need to change their default setting to 'I am not sure if I believe, so convince me; and (2) experience. Both of these settings are where good investigators are."

Yet how do we deal with a spouse or a child whom we think is lying without giving them the FBI shakedown? We certainly aren't trying to lock them up. We're trying to discover the truth and still have a spouse or a child who respects and loves us. It's important to know whether someone is being honest with you, but it's also essential to look closely at the facts before confronting him or her. We want the full truth from our family members, friends, and loved ones. We must remember that in seeking that truth, it is crucial to be diligent, careful, and kind.

Whether we know the truth or need to find it, it is never a good idea to start any conversation with "I know you've lied to me!" That will instantly build a wall between you and the truth. It sets up an innate defense system. Instead, start by asking, "Can we talk about what happened?" and then narrow in, point by point. Remember, as any good investigator will tell you, that if people are lying, they can't remember the smallest details of every lie they've told, so eventually they will snare themselves.

Sometimes the facts are right in front of you: bank accounts don't match what you've been told has been deposited, sales charts at work aren't anywhere near the projections, or you've caught your loved one in a compromising situation. Other trouble is quiet trouble, beneath the surface, and much more subtle.

"Compare how someone acts when telling the truth and how he acts when making a lie," Dr. Dale Archer says. "With a spouse, you know them well. Eye contact is not the same, and your mind goes, 'Warning, warning, danger!' Pay attention to those subtle changes, but remember that a feeling is not enough. You need to confirm it and analyze it in depth."

I often find that the best way to detect lies is with the straight-on, direct question, such as, "Did you do it?" or "What happened to the money?" An alibi is the first thing a cop would ask for—"Where were you last night?"—and then would combine that with the journalist's mantra of who, what, when, where, why, and how.

A "follow trail" is another way to obtain an honest answer. This is a powerful tool that lawyers often use to get to the heart of something. You simply keep asking a question, getting an answer, and then asking the question again. For example, "and?/and?/and?" or "how?/how?/how?" or "why?/why?/why?"

Q: Where were you last night?
A: My friends and I were just hanging out at the mall.
Q: And?
(Pause and wait for an answer.)
A: We were just hanging out at the mall.
Q: And?
A: And we went over to Ricky's.
Q: And?
A: And we hung out.

Q: And?
A: And I had one beer.
Confession. The truth achieved.

Another example is to get the individual you are questioning to agree, agree, and agree until his lie is exposed. I remember a case in which a man involved in a paternity suit was on the stand denying, denying, and denying that he was the father of this woman's child. His claim was that there was no way he should have to pay child support. Throughout the testimony, he had stuck to his well-rehearsed story. Then the mother's attorney asked four questions:

Q: Sir, do you have your wallet with you today?
A: Yes.
Q: Could you take it out for us, please?
A: Yes.
Q: Do you have any pictures in your wallet, sir?
A: (very long pause) Yes.
Q: Could you show them to the jury, please?

The guy carried pictures of the child in his wallet. Game over.

The other classic cross-examination technique is what I call the "Triple C." That is Commit, Credit, Confront. If you know someone is lying to you—if you have the facts—this is a technique to get the person to come clean.

**Commit.** The first step is to get the person to commit to a fact about the lie you know he or she has told. For example, "Yes, I was there at a certain place and time." Or, "Yes, my teacher has said I'm having trouble in class."

**Credit.** You agree with the statement and move the conversation forward. You confirm something that you know is true. For example, "I remember you were out that night." Or, "You have said you've been working extra hard on algebra."

**Confront.** You present the evidence you've garnered, the facts you have. For example, "I know you weren't there because so-and-so saw you elsewhere." Or, "Your teacher called and said you haven't turned in homework for the last two weeks."

Here's how it would work in action:

Q: You went out with the guys on Friday night, right?
A: Yep.
Q: You said Bob, Ted, and Frank?
A: Yes, I did.
Q: And I had my night out with the girls. You went to the Dive Bar on 96th Street?
A: Yes, we did.
Q: Well, I ran into Bob at the post office yesterday, and he asked about you. In fact, he said he hadn't seen you in weeks.

Gulp.

Yet sometimes, because we ourselves may be hurt or the situation may be delicate, we are afraid to ask the hard questions to find out the real answers.

So, how do you get a straight, honest answer from someone?

"We want the full truth from the people we know," William Daly said. "And as the spouse or the parent questioning a family member, it is more difficult than questioning a violent criminal. Why? You have a personal stake in this discussion and, in fact, may well also be the victim. Thus, piercing the 'veil' around the individual and the circumstances may be very difficult because you are bringing into the discussion past elements of the relationship. In addition, the family member or the friend knows the result of the conversation will impact his or her personal relationship with you going forward."

Though difficult, questioning someone you have a personal relationship with will raise any unresolved issues, questions, or concerns, so this will help leverage a satisfactory answer and solution, sooner rather than later. The important thing about questioning someone close to you is to be intuitive about the person you are dealing with and to maintain compassion for him or her. Remember, you will hopefully know your friends, family, and colleagues for a long while, so getting the truth out and up front in any relationship sooner is better. Sometimes it will involve tears and pain, but in the end, knowing the truth will make your bond stronger.

Now, how do we deal with the truth once we know it?

## THE TRUTH ADVANTAGE CHECKUP
### *Set Your Lie-dar*

**When someone is lying, the truth can be discovered in:**

**What the person says.**
- Realize that liars will tend to sound overprepared.
- Know that liars' stories will seem scripted.
- Note that liars pause after being asked a question or they ask the question back to you.

**What the individual's body says.**
- Realize what a suspected liar's normal behavior is.
- Know that a liar's body will give clues that a lie is being told.
- Note that a liar's body will often sweat, twitch, and shift.

**The trail he or she leaves behind.**
- Realize that even the best liars can't keep track of all of their lies.
- Know that with the Internet, everything we do is monitored and tracked.
- Note that a follow trail of questions can often lead to a discovery.

# PART THREE

# The Truth Advantage: The 7 Keys

*The speech of a good person is worth waiting for.*

—PROVERBS 10:20

CHAPTER 6

# Key 1: Look in the Mirror

*Man stands in his own shadow and wonders why
it's dark.*

—ZEN PROVERB

Before you go one sentence further, stop and ask yourself this question: "Whom do I trust?"

Did someone come to mind? Someone who is not just a "yes" person but an honest person? Someone whom you wholeheartedly put your faith in without question, a person who tells you something, and not one iota of doubt about its truthfulness enters your mind? Someone to whom in times of joy and pain you feel safe telling your secrets?

Now, think about the qualities of that person.

In the American Truth Survey of three hundred adults that I conducted for this book, several traits that describe what makes a good friend appeared in responses again and again. Loyalty, honesty, and trust were noted by many participants, as were kindness, reliability, and a sense of humor. Yet what I found so informative was how people elaborated on these specific traits. "A friend will always have your back and never talk behind it," said one respondent. Another said, "Not only will a true friend tell you the truth, but a true friend will expect it from you." And I appreciated the comment from a woman who identified herself as "perpetually single": "A true friend is kind to me, even when I don't deserve it."

"I always size up people this way," ABC *Shark Tank* star Barbara Corcoran told me. "If I left my baby with this person and returned a year later, would my baby be okay? If it's questionable, I know to run the other way."

"There are always rough patches in any relationship," said one insightful survey commentator. "A good sense of humor has saved my friendships more than once. Friends who laugh together, stick together." Agreed. And I've often said, there are those who can laugh and those who can't. I always try to surround myself with friends who can laugh.

These admirable traits and qualities are, of course, desirable to all of us when *choosing* our friends, but how about when they are choosing us? Ask yourself, "Am I the kind of friend I want to have?" "Do my friends know they can trust me?"

Are you the friend whom other friends feel confident and comfortable telling their own truths to? Do people feel safe sharing their secrets with you? Are you trustworthy?

There's an old proverb: "Tell your friend a lie. If he keeps it secret, then tell him the truth." Have you kept your friends' secrets? Do your friends and colleagues know that your words and deeds can be trusted? Have you or do you give anyone reason to doubt you?

Since childhood, we have been told that we should be "good." We are taught that being truthful is good and being dishonest is bad. Yet in our culture, honesty is a value that has in many ways been discarded and whose fundamental importance has been forgotten. It seems that every day we are faced with a well-known person telling a lie or being held accountable for one. Politicians and celebrities' lies unraveling in the public eye and turning into scandals are nothing new. We crucify these people for their dishonesty and hypocrisy, but the reality is that we are all complicit.

As we discovered in part 1, everyone lies. We live in a culture filled with lies, dishonesty, and people saying whatever they have to say to get by and get ahead. We lie to strangers, to our closest friends, and even to ourselves. One of the most revealing things a close friend ever said to me was, "I never told you any lies I didn't tell myself." I had been mad at him, but his confession put his lies into perspective, because we do lie to ourselves and then pass those lies along as truths.

Although people have countless personal reasons for being dishonest, which are specific to various situations, there are also general reasons that most humans are prone to dishonesty. We lie to make ourselves feel good. We lie to avoid certain consequences, from legal troubles to a loved one's disappointment. We lie so that people around us, from new acquaintances to our nearest and dearest, will think highly of us. It's shocking to realize, but we often lie hoping it will help us be liked.

Telling the truth is simple. Telling the truth consistently is tough . . . for all of us. We've each heard and probably told a few whoppers in our day: "The check is in the mail." "I'll call you in the morning." "Let's have lunch." Many of these fall into one of the Triple C's: lies of convenience, congratulations, or consideration. The well-intended compliment, the delicate excuse to get out of a dinner party, the perfunctory "Fine" after "How are you?" We tell these little fibs because it might not be the appropriate time or situation to say, "Your hat is hideous, your food is horrible, and my day stinks."

Have you ever witnessed a child tell the truth in a circumstance where the truth is being avoided? Let me give you an example. I was standing in line at a bookstore behind a young boy and his mother. They were asking the male sales associate behind the desk about where to find a certain children's book. The man was missing his arm and was typing on the computer keyboard using his one hand. The little boy pointed at the man's missing arm and asked, "Where'd your arm go?" Instantly, I felt the mother cringe, as many of us would have done. Her first instinct was to tell her child that the question was inappropriate, that the truth—both the man's and her son's—should be ignored.

The man smiled at the little boy and said, "Kind of you to ask. I was born with only one arm."

"Did it hurt?" the little boy asked.

"Not at all," the man told him.

"I'm glad," the little boy said. They both smiled at each other. And that was it.

It was a question an adult might never have asked. Instead, the adult would have noticed the missing arm, remained quiet, and then wildly speculated as to all of the painful scenarios that might have befallen this man. It was a beautiful moment to witness, though, because it was a pure, well-intended truth, for the boy and for the man. I have to think that both of them were better for it.

Being a mother myself, I'm certain the boy and his mother had a conversation later about what you're "not supposed to ask" people, and the boy was left perplexed and wondering why he shouldn't talk about the truth.

Yet the truth is often more refreshing: "I did it." "This is going to hurt a little." And "Try the other dress." If you feel the need to tell your grandma you like her burnt sweet potato casserole or an acquaintance that her new facelift suits her, Greek philosopher Plato might say go ahead. These "noble lies," as he called them, aren't actively being told to hurt somebody. In fact, the noble lie might be an attempt to make a person's lot in life a little easier.

Communications professor Dr. Mark L. Knapp cuts all of us a little slack. "Technically, one cannot ever be 100 percent honest if that means you tell all that you know about something," he said to me. "So, what it usually means is that you try to get someone else to understand something the way you do. If you can't stand the sweet potatoes, you may rave about the turkey. Or you may say that you really liked the fact that the cook put a lot of brown sugar in the sweet potatoes (which is true, even though you didn't like the dish as a whole). You could also say, 'Overall, I liked some of your dishes, but others I didn't like at all,' which is also true. But your friendship with the cook may take precedence over that form of honesty."

There are ways to deal with these situations more truthfully—while still sparing feelings—that might make life better for everyone. It may be as simple as telling Grandma you like "caramelized" brown sugar or telling your friend that she has a lot to look forward to because you've heard that a facelift looks its best about a year after surgery. Yet even if you said you loved the casserole and the facelift was fabulous, would that be so wrong? Probably not. Both your grandma and your friend went to some effort to achieve their results, and, let's face it, the casserole is cooked and the stitches are out—there is not a whole lot that can be changed in either situation. Furthermore, these things are so minor in the greater scheme of life that it might be better just to let them go.

What you shouldn't do is be cruel to your grandma or your friend or untrue to yourself.

Here's something important to understand in everything you do: In your words and actions, you must remain your authentic self. You must be you. If you're not, you won't be happy, and others will notice.

The great Dr. Seuss said, "Be who you are and say what you feel because those who mind don't matter and those who matter don't mind." Taken out of rhyme, this translates to mean that those who love you want you to be yourself, but they also want you to let them be themselves. Life is a reciprocal relationship, a give and take. One of the greatest and simplest biblical thoughts is to "Love your neighbor as yourself." How do we all want to be loved? We want to be accepted, honored, and cherished. We want to be liked, trusted, and adored. And how can you be these things for others, if you aren't these things for yourself? How can you love others, if you don't love yourself? You can't.

So, it all begins with you.

Loving yourself is accepting your imperfections but working toward improving yourself as well. Loving yourself means making the most of your life's path but being willing to change course when necessary. Loving yourself is when your head and your heart agree with what's coming out of your mouth.

Yes, being you takes courage, but with nothing to hide, you have nothing to fear.

Ellen DeGeneres comes to mind as a great example of someone who dealt with her authentic truth and rose to the top. In April 1997, her character Ellen "came out of the closet" on her sitcom and announced to her friends that she was a lesbian. It was groundbreaking television. She landed on the cover of *Time* magazine with the headline: "Yep, I'm Gay." In doing so, she lost her entire career. She was called "Ellen Degenerate." She was threatened. She went through a major depression. And then her truth telling did something interesting; it helped her find herself and start again. She's now at the top of her game, hosting a beloved, highly rated talk show; married to the beautiful Portia de Rossi; and an icon of beauty as the spokesperson for Cover Girl. This is a profound, real-world example of how personal honesty leads to happiness and fulfillment.

On telling the truth, Ellen DeGeneres told *Glamour* magazine, "Find out who you are and be that person. That's what your soul was put on this earth to be. Find that truth, live that truth, and everything else will come." Being honest and forthright is respected and liberating. In a world where so many lies are layered on us every day, when someone is being real, it is both alluring and refreshing. It's hard not to like her.

Other celebrities have, of course, shown us what not to do. They've hidden their truths and fallen from grace. Why? We felt betrayed, just as their partners did. Tiger Woods and Jesse James both allowed personal betrayals to become full-out, destructive scandals, and each reminded me of the old saying: "You can't hide from the truth." You can run, but you can't hide. If you're inauthentic, it catches up with you and nips at your heels.

The truth starts with each of us, within each of us. We can live it, be it, and achieve it. Or not. The choice of an authentic life is solely ours.

We come into this world with nothing, and we go out the same way. In between, our good name is all we've got. If, in being yourself, you're consistently spinning stories, being hurtful, or doing wrong, realize that people notice. If you're known as the guy who tries to pull the wool over people's eyes with sneaky tactics and verbal gymnastics, or the guy who tries to put people down, thinking you'll rise above, you're not the guy who is fondly remembered. You're also not the guy whom people turn to with their respect, their business, or their love. If you're not living honestly, be aware that others are on to you.

In your relationships with others, if you're not true to the commitments you have made, you are not being genuine. That disingenuousness is a wedge between your real self and the phony self, the façade that you're creating. If that's the case, most people can feel that something is amiss. Your friends, coworkers, children, and partners probably know you well enough to intuitively feel that you're not being totally honest. How many times have you been asked or asked someone else, "Is everything okay?"

What's great about being your authentic self is that it relieves you of the guilt of not being perfect. Perhaps nothing is a healthier realization. As Dr. Seuss said, "Today you are YOU, that is truer than true. There is no one alive who is Youer than You." The truth is you can't be anything but you, so make the most of it. Do I dislike that I'm a divorced woman? Yes. Am I ever grateful that my marriage gave me my kids? Yes! Self-doubts are erased, and you achieve a defined clarity when you recognize that the very real life you have is the one you're supposed to have. If you're being truthful, you are living the life you should be living.

As an added bonus, being authentically you allows you to answer honestly but confidently. "Is that your real hair color?" "Yes, it's my real hair color." (It may be bottle blonde, but it's really the color on my head.) "How much did you pay for that?" "My mother would be shocked, my dad would be proud." (Whether too much or too little, it's none of your business.) "How old are you?" "Hopefully, younger than I look. Certainly, older than I feel." (In other words, how dare you!)

---

TRUTH ADVANTAGE DO'S AND DON'TS!

DO go for your own personal best.
DON'T criticize yourself for every flaw.

---

What questions do we ask to find out whether we are really being honest, even with ourselves? How do we harness our true selves?

We all know what we want, need, and expect from other people. Following a fight with a significant other, how many of us have thought, "I wish my husband would just do ____" or

"Why can't my children just do ____?" What do we want from ourselves, though? Often, we are quick to judge others with a critical eye for behavior that we ourselves may very well be guilty of, or we expect qualities in others that we ourselves lack. This goes for many qualities, but especially one that should be at the foundation of every relationship we have: honesty.

How many of us react in hurt or anger when confronting someone in our lives with a lie, even if it is harmless? I can recall one time when, at the very last minute, a friend canceled plans to spend time with me, saying she was sick. "Okay, that's perfectly reasonable," I thought, understanding why she canceled. A few days later, I found out she had actually spent time with another friend instead. When I asked her about it, she apologized and explained that she was just getting over an argument with this friend and that they had gotten together to work things out.

The real reason made sense, of course, but it still bothered me. What about our friendship or me made her think I wouldn't accept the truth? Had she simply told me the truth, I would have been much more sympathetic. Wouldn't I? Instead, I felt that her dishonesty had caused a ripple of hurt in our friendship. I was annoyed. Should I not trust her? Could she not trust me?

This circumstance really gave me pause to think about my own behavior in the past. I, too, have done similar things under similar circumstances. Yet I was too busy being angry with my friend to think about my own behavior, to look at myself.

That's where self-reflection and self-awareness come in.

As Norman Vincent Peale said, "One of the greatest moments in anybody's developing experience is when he no longer tries to hide from himself but determines to get acquainted with himself as he really is." Self-reflection is the act of truly facing yourself, honestly thinking about who you are and who you want to be and the changes that build the bridge between them.

It's not necessarily easy. As Cassandra, a sixty-year-old in Oklahoma, pointed out on the American Truth Survey, "I know when I'm being totally honest with myself because I find myself cringing."

Psychologist Allen R. McConnell wrote on his *Psychology Today* blog, "Change requires two things: a goal, and an awareness of where one currently is in order to assess the discrepancy between the two. In short, we cannot reach our destinations without knowledge of our current location on the map." Self-reflection gives us a chance to really see who we are and gain crucial self-awareness, without which we cannot grow.

Self-reflection isn't necessarily easy because it requires dealing with parts of ourselves that we may not be proud of. As the ToDo Institute (a nonprofit educational retreat center for mental wellness) states, "A sincere examination of ourselves is not an easy task. It requires attention to what has not been attended to. It involves a willingness to squarely face our mistakes, failure and weakness . . . to acknowledge our transgressions and actions which have caused difficulty to others." The effort of self-reflection requires taking the time to question and evaluate who we are and what values we represent. The insight gained through the process is invaluable.

Before we can demand things from other people, we first have to evaluate ourselves. And as Ralph Waldo Emerson said, "He who is not everyday conquering some fear has not learned the secret of life." Are you who you want to be? Do you do things that you expect others to do? Do you tell the truth to yourself? This is not about becoming a constant nag or beating yourself up for every minor flaw. Instead, as the old saying goes, it's about "knowing thyself." When you know yourself, you are fairly assessing your feelings, your behavior, and your sensitivity to others and seeing how you might adjust the characteristics you are unhappy with.

Mahatma Gandhi reminded us, "A man of truth must also be a man of care." We must first realize that we're always a work in progress. Each of us is a constantly changing organism with diverse emotions, attitudes, and feelings. But getting to our core values—what we are, what we want, and how we want to be—is the secret to an honest, truthful life. As Joseph Campbell says, "Follow your bliss."

Our busy lives often make us lose touch with honesty and truthfulness. When you make self-reflection a priority and then take positive steps toward becoming more truthful, you are more likely to receive the truth from others. Being aware of your own personality, your likes and dislikes and strengths and weaknesses, enables you to deal with anything that is thrown your way. In addition, you'll gain a kindness toward, and respect of, others' personalities and their strengths and weaknesses. Having a clear perception of yourself—from beliefs to motivation—allows you to understand others and enables you to give an honest, appropriate response in the moment, whatever that moment may be.

Think back to that person you thought of at the beginning of this chapter: the friend, the colleague, or the loved one you turn to in time of need; the person you trust with your secrets; the person you put your faith in. This is a person who cares, who loves you as he loves himself. If you ever have a day when you don't feel like being kind, being honest, or being a caring soul, think of that friend.

Action follows intent. Intend yourself to be honest, and you will work toward being honest. You'll be as honest as you make up your mind to be.

Chapters 7 through 12 describe the next six keys to The Truth Advantage that will help you get there.

## THE TRUTH ADVANTAGE CHECKUP
### "Mirror, Mirror, on the Wall . . ."

**Figure out the "why."**

- Realize that you are who you are for a reason.
- Take some time to really understand why you do what you do and say what you say.
- Know that why you act a certain way will help you avoid repeating old patterns in future behavior.
- History is the best predictor of the future.

**Forgive yourself for past mistakes.**

- Realize that you don't have to beat yourself up.
- Take note that self-reflection is not about viewing who you are with judgmental eyes.
- Know that in looking at yourself, it's all about admitting that yes, you've made mistakes, but you want to do better.

**Find your own role model.**

- Keep in mind a friend you admire for being truthful who will inspire you to become a better, more truthful you.
- Name the specific qualities that you admire in this person.
- Learn from this person's attributes and behavior to positively change your own.
- Write your own epitaph, the words you want friends to describe you with when you're no longer around.

# CHAPTER 7

# Key 2: Listen Up!

*To listen well is as powerful a means of influence as to
talk well, and is as essential to all true conversation.*

—CHINESE PROVERB

Perhaps the greatest of all human desires is to be heard. Yet if
you're like me, you've had to ask friends, colleagues, and
partners on numerous occasions, "Are you listening to me?"
Why? Too often, as is human nature, we're more interested in
ourselves than in anyone else. To borrow the question asked
once by a yoga instructor: "Are we listening, or are we just waiting for our turn to speak?"

What I often found in the courtroom was that rather than
listening, many trial attorneys would put someone on the stand
and ask a list of prepared questions by rote. They would ask
question after question without carefully listening and adapt-
ing their line of questioning to what was being said. Let me give
you an example. I remember being a newbie prosecutor and

watching as my opposing counsel put an elderly lady on the stand as a witness. After she had taken the oath to tell the truth, he requested that she give her name, address, and birth date. When she said the date, it was evident that she was off by several decades. I noted both the error and several jurors' puzzled expressions, but my opposing counsel just plowed ahead with his other questions. Why? He wasn't really listening. The witness wasn't intentionally lying. She was nervous and, in her nervousness, had gotten her dates mixed up.

When it came my turn to question the witness, I opened my questions a bit more personally, "Ma'am, is this the first time you've testified in court?"

"Yes," she answered.

"Are you nervous?"

"Yes."

"You indicated you were born in 1973. Is that correct?"

"Oh, goodness no," she laughed. "1937! Thank you for checking!" By listening to her, I gained not only her trust, but also the trust of the jury.

Now, every day on TV, I sit opposite people who are paid to argue with me. They come onto the set ready to rumble and have their points so well memorized that they deliver them and fail to even listen to what I'm saying. I've found that I often have the leg up because my trial by fire in the courtroom trained me to give people the floor to talk and to actually listen to what was being said, before I presented the truth of my case. Inevitably, I discovered that even though they were of the opposite opinion, many of the opposing attorneys respected that I listened to them, and as a result, it helped me win my case. The people you listen to are quite simply more likely to want to help you achieve your goals.

Dale Carnegie, the author of the perennial bestseller *How to Win Friends and Influence People*, suggested that the ability to listen is the rarest of good traits, but the skill can carry you further than any other. He noted that the *Reader's Digest* once pointed out, "Many persons call a doctor when all they want is an audience." There's even a syndrome called "Munchausen by proxy," in which an individual—usually, a mother—deliberately makes another person sick (most often, her own child) to gain attention and sympathy from doctors. This illness, named after Baron von Munchausen, an eighteenth-century German dignitary known for telling tall tales, is one of the most harmful forms of child abuse and comes directly from the desire to be listened to.

Dale Carnegie suggested that the quickest way to get anyone to like you is to be a good listener because everyone wants to be heard. Carnegie said that a winning secret of success was to encourage people you're with to talk about themselves, "because the man you are talking to is a hundred times more interested in himself and his wants and his problems than he is in you and your problems." If you really want to get someone on your team, encourage him to talk about himself. "To be interesting, be interested."

"I find that no one in my life really listens to me," Evelyn, a fifty-two-year-old woman from Arizona, confessed in the comment section of the American Truth Survey. "It seems to me that everyone is so busy with their own lives today that people never really make time to just be with someone."

Do you take the time to listen to others? Well, you should. As Bernard M. Baruch observed, "Most of the successful people I've known are the ones who do more listening than talking." Psychologists point out that your "likeability quotient" is high if people feel as if they are being heard. In television, your likeability quotient is called your "Q Rating." At first I thought that meant, *Do people like what I'm saying? Like how I look?* Yet I've come to realize that the Q Rating has more to do with whether viewers understand that I'm really listening, really tuning in to what the person on the opposite side of the debate is saying to me, and am I responding in kind to what's been said, or just reading off prompter cards.

In life, if someone thinks you're listening to him, he automatically tends to like you. By becoming a good listener, you will improve your chances of persuading, influencing, and dealing successfully with others. The International Listening Association says that after more than thirty-five business studies were conducted, listening proved to be the top skill needed to form a solid relationship. Studies on positive parenting reveal that if kids know they are being heard, they are in turn more likely to listen to what their parents are saying.

Listening is a compelling skill. A good listener flatters his subject without having to say a word. People are drawn toward people who listen as iron is drawn to a magnet. So, no matter what truth you have to tell other people, if they believe they are being listened to and heard first, they will be far more likely to be amenable when you present your truth.

The art of listening is the age-old secret of survivors. There were once two cavemen out walking in the woods. One caveman was talking; the other was listening. The talker was blabbering on and on about his wife's snoring, his kids not doing their chores, the mortgage on his cave, and other mundane caveman topics. The listener was listening well and heard his friend's drivel, as well as the movement in the bushes. Let's just say, the listener made it home. The talker met a hungry saber-toothed tiger. Good listening hasn't changed: he who listens best not only survives but succeeds.

I once heard my friend tell her snappish daughter, "You're not hard of hearing; you're hard of listening." There's an important distinction between hearing and listening. Unless you're hearing-impaired, hearing happens easily. The ear perceives sound without any effort on your part. Listening, on the other hand, does take effort. You have to consciously choose to listen.

Listening requires your brain to process sounds into words and words into sentences. We learn by listening.

Perfecting the skill of good listening gives you a real advantage by increasing your respectability and your chance of finding out what you need to know to achieve the best results. When you learn how to listen carefully, not only do others think of you kindly, but you also get to bank fundamental, often crucial, information that will help you make important decisions. The truism "information is power" shows that the single best route to gaining information is through listening.

In short, good listening is the first step to gaining the edge in all that you do.

---

TRUTH ADVANTAGE DO'S AND DON'TS!

DO pay attention with your whole being.
DON'T think that throwing out an occasional "uh huh" and a
    nod of your head is listening.

---

Several studies suggest that we absorb only 25 to 50 percent of what we hear. Think about what this means—that's a whole lot of missed details and items of significance. On a daily basis, you're talking to your boss, your colleagues, your spouse, your children, and your customers, and you remember only one-quarter to one-half of what they've told you. That is an abysmal record, and I'd be willing to bet it is certain to cause trouble in more than a few relationships.

When we listen poorly, we do more than miss crucial information being shared by the person speaking; we also raise the chances that the relationship won't last. We might think we're clever enough to "tune out" during a conversation and then "tune in" without the other person noticing our lack of attention, but we're not.

Think about it. Don't you recognize when someone isn't really focused on what you're saying during a conversation? You, like me, have probably heard the mind-numbing "uh-huh" while you're speaking or when you're asked a question that you already answered a few minutes prior. You, like me, have probably seen people's eyes glaze over as you're talking to them or, worse, caught them looking over your shoulder to see who else in the room might be worth talking to. Bottom line: we have a hunch when someone isn't really listening. And you've probably asked yourself, "Am I really that boring?" Yes, in some cases, we're all boring. In most situations, though, it's probably more likely that the person listening to you has just let his or her mind wander elsewhere, into private thoughts, needs, and desires.

"Deep listening is miraculous for both listener and speaker," said Sue Patton Thoele, the author of *The Mindful Woman: Gentle Practices for Restoring Calm, Finding Balance & Opening Your Heart*. "When someone receives us with open-hearted, non-judging, intensely interested listening, our spirits expand."

We expect—and need—the people close to us to truly listen when we speak, whether we are sharing our joys or our sorrows, good ideas or bad. When someone we're talking with doesn't listen, we can't help but feel hurt and wonder why the person didn't feel it was worth his or her time to pay attention. Listening to people share their thoughts is not only a way of connecting with them, but also a way to show that we care about their thoughts and feelings. Why would we want to spend time with someone who doesn't care for us?

By not listening, you're doing more than wasting someone's time—you're communicating that the person isn't worth your attention. Although that may not be your intent, a relationship cannot thrive if there isn't mutual respect or care between both individuals. Without those elements, no meaningful relationship can blossom.

Why don't we listen? Well, first off, modern society provides us with a lot of distractions. A newly popular one is texting. According to the A. C. Nielsen Co., the average teenager sends more than three thousand texts per month. That's more than six texts per waking hour. More than once, I've had to tell my two teenagers to stop texting while they were having a serious conversation with me. Then there's the computer. Nielsen found that the typical Facebook user spends an average of 421 minutes per month on the site, which amounts to more than 14 minutes per day.

People often confess to multitasking while talking on the phone. In one online poll, 80 percent of people admitted that they "occasionally" use the computer while talking on the phone, while more than half had serious conversations while doing something else "regularly." (I confess that I am one of the 80 percent, often returning e-mails while talking on the phone.) Then there's the TV. According to Nielsen, the TV is on an average of six hours and forty-seven minutes a day in the average U.S. home. That's basically from the time we get up until we leave for work and most of the hours from when we get home until we go to bed. We might be having conversations, but our background is often swirling with news, commercials, and characters from housewives to quarterbacks who claim our attention. How could we not get distracted?

Even the places that are supposed to offer us a respite from distraction need to make a point to remind us. If you ever go to the theater or the opera, it's so rare that you can enjoy the event without distractions. Now my gym has even instituted a no cell phone policy. Its sign says "Can you hear me now?" with an X through a cell phone. We've all heard that annoying piercing call that we don't want to hear but are forced to overhear. And, by the way, let me take this opportunity to point out if you're sitting with someone at dinner, unless your kid is bleeding from the head, let the texting or the calling wait. It's such a disrespectful thing to do to someone sitting across from you. Don't put the human being with you on hold for someone who isn't.

In addition to distractions, there are other habits that promote poor listening. "My mother is a terrible listener," complained a friend of mine. "We've gotten into fights over it. She'll act as if she's listening, but she's totally looking through me. I'll tell her something to her face, like I'm going out or away on a trip, and when I leave, she'll scream at me and tell me I didn't tell her. It's really frustrating. Reeeeeally frustrating. It makes me not want to tell her anything because it doesn't matter anyway. It is definitely detrimental to our having a good relationship."

My friend is not alone. Many of the people I interviewed and surveyed said that they often feel not heard, although several also came clean about their own bad listening habits, admitting they were often unaware of what someone had been saying for the last five minutes because they had "tuned out." Or, as one man put it, "The truth is that some people I have to talk to on a daily basis are really boring, mind-numbingly boring. I have to find something else to think about while they're talking or I might go crazy."

If that isn't bad enough, many of us are listening only to hear a thought to disagree or argue with. When we finally hear something we disagree with, we get stuck on it and stop listening well. Every word out of that person's mouth then turns into a muted hum in our ears. We're not listening to the conversation; we're formulating our next argument. A good listener attempts to understand what someone is saying, and although he might disagree with what's being said, because he's listened carefully, he knows exactly what he's disagreeing with.

Why should you learn to be a better listener? In addition to being more popular, you might actually learn something! If information is power, the best way to gain information is by listening.

The great writer Ernest Hemingway said, "I like to listen. I have learned a great deal from listening carefully. Most people never listen." I learned in the courtroom that by careful and attentive listening, I learned crucial information, both through what was said and what wasn't said. By actively listening, I won cases. By listening well, you gain important knowledge that will help you or those you love when it really matters. I love this quote by Edward Hersey Richards: "A wise old owl sat on an oak; The more he saw the less he spoke; The less he spoke the more he heard; Why aren't we like that wise old bird?"

We're attracted to those wise old birds. I have my "silent treatment test." I find that I can sit in a room with the people I most trust and love and be comfortable in the silence, without a need to fill in the gaps. Just try it sometime. There's often beauty in the silence.

"Stop talking and let the other person talk," Dr. Dale Archer advises. "If there is a pause, don't rush to fill it. Allow the other to talk. Often what he says right after a pause, when most folks feel uncomfortable, is important and telling."

When a good listener hears us, our lives expand. Good listening is an acknowledgment that we matter. As an aside, how many of your friends' birthdays do you acknowledge with a call, a card, or a gift, and how many of your friends make a celebratory moment out of your birthday? When someone recognizes your special day, it makes you feel good. I know it makes me happy. The same is true with listening. When people feel listened to, they feel good. They feel valued, heard, and understood. Making others feel good will enrich your life, and the mutual benefit is a more honest, truthful relationship.

Yes, on occasion, let's admit it, people may have stories that are too long or too boring, or that concern something we have no interest in. I've been at many a dinner party where the person next to me talked on and on about kid problems, work minutiae, and even stomach ailments, but I listened. Why? It was respectful, and in return I received respect. As an added bonus, when I'm listening to someone drone on and on, it serves as a reminder for me of what *not* to do to the next person I speak to.

Listening is a crucial skill in the ladder of life. We listen to learn, to understand, and for enjoyment. By listening to others, you are communicating that you respect them and value what they say. When we turn off and stop listening, we are putting up a wall. If we become distracted or focused on our own agendas, we are losing our bond with another person.

How good of a listener you are will have a major impact on your life, whether at work or at home. Being a good listener will improve your friendships and your relationships and will buoy your career. Why? Because by making people feel good, you earn their trust.

Let it be known that most people *think* they are good listeners. In actuality, they may have good hearing, but they are poor listeners. There's a key difference between hearing and listening. We're born with the ability to hear, but listening is an acquired skill. Many of us fail to develop good listening skills, despite years of conversing with others. So, after all of these years of habitually waiting for our turn to speak, how do we become good listeners? How do we gain that advantage?

Old habits die hard. If you haven't been listening, really listening, in a while, it will take some work to break that bad habit.

Here are some basic points to remember about good listening that I learned in the courtroom.

### The keys to being a great listener:

- **Don't interrupt**. The first and most important aspect of listening well is not interrupting while someone is talking. If you do, it's a sign that you are not listening and are wasting that person's time. Furthermore, if you're speaking, you're not adding anything to your wealth of knowledge, packing anything in your suitcase. You aren't learning. Whenever an attorney in the courtroom repeatedly interrupted someone, I always watched the jury. They were never pleased. It made that attorney instantly disliked and put a strike against his case. The same is true if you're constantly interrupting a spouse or a work colleague. It makes the person far less likely to listen to you and your desires when it's your time to speak.

- **Avoid distractions.** When someone is speaking to you, ignore the phone, stop texting, turn off the TV, and put yourself in a place as free of extraneous noise as possible. If something interrupts or you do find yourself distracted, ask the person you're speaking with to repeat himself or ask whether you could call him back. These small courtesies tell the speaker you want to hear everything he's saying, while also ensuring that you don't miss something important.

- **Actively listen.** Listening isn't passive. When you're really listening to someone, you are putting your thoughts aside and becoming fully engaged with what the other person says. In short, you are "with" the other person. Let someone know you're listening by nodding, by saying "yes," and by maintaining good eye contact and posture. Here's a listening tip a debate coach once taught me: press the tip of your tongue behind your front teeth. He said it stops internal dialogue. Try it. I used it in the courtroom anytime I found myself getting distracted or not in the moment with what the speaker was saying.

- **Don't offer advice.** Although I'm always asked for my legal advice at every cocktail party, I've found that people are rarely seeking advice. They often just need a sounding board. They need someone to listen to them. Don't mistake the desire to share something with you as a cry for a psychological examination or a desire for a life critique.

Attempting to psychoanalyze people or explain their own feelings to them will only lead to their cutting you off. Show those who are speaking that their feelings are valid by simply listening to what they have to say.

- **Show appreciation.** When people share their stories or feelings with you, and you let them know that you feel honored by their trust, you earn their respect. You want the people you encounter to feel validated. When they do, they feel both heard and understood. I learned that by not passing judgment on what someone is saying—whether it be opposing counsel or political pundits—I become more likable. Instead, I accept that opinions can be opposite of my own, and I find something in the exchange to appreciate. This doesn't mean you have to agree with all of their points—you'll never think or feel exactly as someone else does—but finding something to agree with is an inroad to having a positive exchange of ideas.

- **Listen between the lines.** When people speak, there are thoughts and concerns beneath and behind what they say. Most people, for example, don't come right out and say, "I'm mad at you." Instead, that subtext might be revealed in what's not being said. If you've ever been in a relationship, you know these not-so-subtle hints can come in the form of a huff, a sideways glance, or a frown. If you've ever talked to a car dealer, a little clue that the price could be lowered may come not in what's he's saying, but by the fact that he's constantly looking over at his manager. When you are listening intently, you are aware of not only what's being said, but also the overall feeling of what's being conveyed. Failure to pick up on these hints and sentiments may leave you in the dark about what's really going on.

- **Understand, then be understood.** When someone finishes talking, make sure you understand what's been said. If you have any doubts, ask for clarification. Always respond to what has been said, rather than trying to change the subject. Don't just listen with the intent of replying as soon as possible; rather, listen with the intent of fully understanding what is being said. Making someone feel understood is one of the most fulfilling aspects of communicating with others. Acknowledging and understanding how someone else feels allows you to truly connect and forge a strong relationship with another human being.

Philosopher Paul Tillich once said, "The first duty of love is to listen." Yet in a recent Associated Press poll, one-third of married women said that their pets listen to them better than their husbands do. That reminds me of something once said by Margo Kaufman: "I would be willing to bet that if one day a woman walked barefoot to the moon and back and a man cleaned out his desk, when the two of them sat down to dinner that night he would say, 'Boy, was that desk a mess!'" Yet communicating is a two-way street. As relationship counselor Dr. John Gray explained in his best-selling book *Men Are from Mars, Women Are from Venus*, there are distinct differences in the sexes, and the solution is rather simple: we must acknowledge and accept these differences before we can develop happy relationships. I'll take it one step further, though, and suggest that we must also learn how to listen to each other. To not be heard can be frustrating for either sex.

"When my husband is really listening to me," said one woman on the survey, "I feel as if he truly loves me. Unfortunately, when he typically listens to me is after we've had a huge fight, and we've both gotten to our breaking point. It's finally then that I realize he does care about what I say. I wish there was a secret to getting to that point without all the drama on a more regular basis."

I've heard that all relationship problems come down to issues in communication. There's a big difference between talking to someone who is listening to understand you and talking to someone who is waiting until it's his turn to argue with you. Relationship experts suggest that instead of formulating a response to someone's point, formulate a question. Rather than poking at what he or she is saying, ask a question that invites the person to share more personal thoughts. "Would you like to make a date to call your mother on Wednesday nights?" The result will often be an improvement in the tone and in the relationship. If you really care for people, when you ask a question, you want to understand what they mean when they answer and not merely hear what they are saying.

Often, the solution to our problems in communicating with anyone, particularly those we are close to or intimate with, is that we need to speak less and listen more. On a side note, I believe that if more Democrats and Republicans would follow this simple directive, we'd get a lot more done and have a much more amiable society—but that discussion is for another day.

Kids are no different than adults (or than Republicans and Democrats, for that matter!). Ranting and raving at them won't get you very far, but listening to them will get you respect. Authors Adele Faber and Elaine Mazlish wrote the classic parenting book *How to Talk So Kids Will Listen & Listen So Kids Will Talk*, in which they point out that nobody likes to be told what to do, but when children (and adults) feel understood, listened to, and respected, they feel better and they act better. And they like you more.

I've learned that the secret of good listening as a parent (or as a friend) is to slow down for a few minutes and take the time to be with my children. Sounds easy, right? It's not. It takes a lot of effort after a day of work and go, go, go for my brain to switch gears, stop thinking about all of the other stuff floating around in there, and give my kids the full attention they deserve. But I've learned to, and, in return, my kids listen to me.

As a parent, if you're doing all of the talking, even if it's what needs to be said, you're missing something crucial from them: understanding. That's the distinction between hearing and listening. It's easy to nod along to your kid's story while you pay bills or make dinner, but are you really listening to what he or she is saying? Careful listening is an essential part of building trust. If you show your kids that you're paying attention, truly listening and interested in their lives when they're young, they will feel much more comfortable talking honestly with you, not only now, but as they grow into adults as well.

Robert Conklin, the author of *How to Get People to Do Things*, said, "Very few people would listen if they didn't know it was their turn next." It's a universal truth: we are naturally always going to be more interested in ourselves than in anyone else. Yet we can improve our lives (and those of others) by learning to improve our listening skills. The payoff for the hard work is great. When we listen with care, compassion, and an open mind, the reward is a blossoming of mutual respect. When you earn another's confidence, you develop a relationship that is comforting, trusting, and available. When you listen with an open mind, new ideas are revealed, and often things that were purposely hidden are illuminated. By knowing where someone is coming from, you can be open and honest. When someone is listened to, he feels his needs are taken into account and will then be far more likely to give you his cooperation and love.

In any situation, if you listen well, you're going to start with an important truth advantage: the trust of others. With your spouse, you will receive more compassion and understanding. With your kids, you will get more cooperation and respect. At work, you will find that if you're listening to others, they are listening to you. In those on-the-job relationships, great ideas will bloom, more work will get done, and your colleagues will look up to you.

As we move forward, just remember an old adage I recall my grandmother saying: "Your ears will never get you into trouble."

Now that you're "all ears," the next step is learning how to get your facts straight.

---

### THE TRUTH ADVANTAGE CHECKUP
#### *Hello? Hello? Can You Hear Me Now?*

**Shut up! (Just for a second.)**

- Realize that before you can listen to someone else, you actually have to stop talking first!
- In the next conversation you have with someone, take note of how much you say, as opposed to how much you listen.
- Know that if you can't remember the last thing the other person said, you've been speaking too long!

**Listen, even when you want to argue.**

- Even if a conversation is making you frustrated or annoyed or leads to smoke pouring out of your ears, don't start talking right away.
- Take three deep breaths through your nose, rather than opening your mouth.
- Know that if you start arguing before someone's finished, you're jumping into a hole that will be hard to climb out of.

**You want to be popular, don't you?**

- Realize that the more you listen to what others have to say, the more respected and liked you will be.
- Take note that no one likes a blabbermouth! Sometimes silence is golden.
- Know that actively listening to someone will ensure a high probability that in return, that person will actually listen to you, too.

# CHAPTER 8

# Key 3: Get Your Facts Straight

*Measure thrice before you cut once.*

—DUTCH PROVERB

o you remember the series *Dragnet* and the great line delivered by Detective Sergeant Joe Friday: "Just the facts, ma'am"?

Well, guess what? Friday, portrayed by actor Jack Webb, never actually said those words. Yep, that's the fact, ma'am. That phrase was actually popularized by the *Dragnet* parodies of comedian Stan Freberg, something I discovered while researching this chapter. In an early episode, Joe Friday did, however, say, "All we want are the facts." Getting the facts is a key step on your way to The Truth Advantage.

Gathering "evidence"—facts and research material—was crucial in every one of my cases and, similarly, will support you in any personal or professional issue. If you want to confidently tell the truth, you can rely on Sergeant Joe Friday's thought: "All we want are the facts." Standing on a foundation of facts that are proved to be truths cannot be argued or denied. It gives you credibility and strength. It will help you know the truth and present it, whether to your kids, your spouse, or your coworkers.

I recently watched my neighbor's Labrador resolutely dig through mounds of snow. I could tell by his frantic movements that he was definitely looking for something. He would work anxiously for a while, tire out, then change his location and strategy of attack and dig again. He eventually discovered a large bone. The effort clearly paid off.

Likewise, getting the facts takes a little extra effort, but the rewards are great. Before you deliver the truth to anybody for any reason, you must know the facts. As I learned in the courtroom, when you're prepared with the facts for any case, you are less likely to veer into the unknown or let your emotions get the best of you, and you are more likely to achieve positive results and gain credibility. When you're backed by facts, you are not only stronger in making your case, you are also more persuasive. The facts give you confidence, wisdom, and power.

So, what are facts? And how *do* we get them?

According to the *Merriam-Webster* dictionary, a fact has the "quality of being actual"; it is "something that has actual existence" and is "presented as having objective reality." Jawaharial Nehru, a statesman and the longest-serving prime minister of India, once said, "Facts are facts and will not disappear on account of your likes." Simply put, opinions can run like wild gazelles; facts are as solid as a rock. Facts don't change according to whom you're speaking. With facts, something happened or it didn't; it's a confirmed statistic or a completely validated and researched piece of information. Facts don't sway with the wind as palm trees do. They don't give in to our manipulations or rationalizations, and they certainly aren't based on our personal perspectives. Facts remain the same, regardless of perception, feeling, or thought.

Examples of facts: If you're trying to talk your way out of a ticket, batting your eyelashes isn't going to change the fact that a stop sign means stop, which you didn't do. If you're a size 16, jumping up and down won't help you squeeze into a size 4. Two atoms of hydrogen and one atom of oxygen bond together to form one molecule of water. No matter how you shake it, it won't become wine.

When I was around eight, I remember riding in the car with my mom and my grandmother. We saw a man lying in a ditch on the side of the road. That was a fact. There was much speculation and discussion as to what he was doing there and what we should do. "Is he hurt?" "Is he a bum?" "Is he dead?" "Does he need help?" My mom, at the wheel, thought we should go back and help, but my grandmother said it could be dangerous. So my mom drove directly to the police station, where she explained that we had seen a man lying in the ditch on Mill Road right across from the old water tower. The police found the man and discovered that he had, in fact, drunk a little too much whiskey at the local bar.

A man lying in a gutter is not necessarily a bum. One person might assume that he is a drunken bum, and another might assume that he's a man who needs help. Assumptions aren't facts. Assumptions are based on each individual's viewpoint and life circumstances. You might have heard the old adage "Don't assume. It makes an ass of 'u' and me."

Let's talk about how to gather our facts.

Though I have my ideas about right and wrong and my theories about what may or may not be, my beliefs are not necessarily facts. Our ideas are intangible. Facts are tangible, and getting to them requires a little work, a little extra effort.

I remember when my son was in kindergarten, and he came home and complained that he didn't have homework. He wanted homework like the "big kids." Then, when he started getting homework in third grade, he began to complain that he didn't want to do it; he wanted to go out and play. Homework doesn't stop when we're out of school. If we want The Truth Advantage, we need to do our homework on a daily basis—whether at work or at home.

When I'm lecturing my law students, I always explain that "discovery" is crucial before you go out and "practice" (and all practicing lawyers know we're always practicing). If you don't have the facts, you will not have the case advantage. You will, in fact, be relinquishing the upper hand. Without the facts, you've set yourself up for failure.

I learned the importance of fact gathering during my first trial as a federal prosecutor. The defendant, John Edward Miller, had been accused of multiple armed robberies, during which he would enter a bank and start shooting at the ceiling. He'd then round up all of the bank employees and lock them in the bank vault, with the exception of one, whom he would make gather the money and stuff it into his bags. During the course of a few years, he would be accused of netting more than a million dollars in his robberies.

I had no direct evidence. I had no eyewitnesses because the disguise worn in all of the bank robberies was fairly standard "bank robber chic": a black nylon stocking over his face and a ski cap. All of my evidence was circumstantial, and, as I tell my students, circumstantial evidence is like a trail of cookie crumbs left on the countertop—a good defense attorney is going to say, "My client didn't eat your cookies. You have mice."

Let me give you another example of circumstantial evidence. Suppose there's been a drought. Your lawn is drier than the desert. You wake up one morning and discover that your yard is flooded, soaked with water. You will assume that while you were sleeping, it rained. The evidence is pretty good, but it's circumstantial. Couldn't a leaky hose be a possible explanation? Until you confirm it with someone who saw the rain or with the National Weather Service, which logged the rain on radar, it's only circumstantial evidence. The facts are theories built on the information you have.

Just as it is in the courtroom, it is dangerous to use circumstantial evidence as your sole source in drawing conclusions about truth in your own life. Let's suppose you come home and discover your favorite heirloom vase broken in pieces on the floor. The only person home between the time you left and the time you returned to find it broken on the floor was your housekeeper. Based on this circumstantial evidence, you naturally jump to the conclusion that your housekeeper broke your favorite vase. And then Muffin the cat walks on by.

In order to support your circumstantial evidence, you need cold, hard facts. Was there an eyewitness who watched the housekeeper knock the vase off? No. Can you see wet paw prints walking away from the seen of the crime? Yes.

For my first trial, I was stuck with a whole lot of circumstantial evidence, which a juror or any otherwise thoughtful person might piece together to form a conclusion. I had an ex-girlfriend's testimony that during each of the bank robberies, Miller was "at work." On the other hand, I had a bank teller, a former shoe salesperson, describe the shoes worn by the bank robber, which happened to be the exact brand and size Miller had on when he was arrested. Yet in addition to that circumstantial evidence, I also found one inarguable fact that convinced the jury and helped me win the case.

I did my homework on Miller. I found out everything I could about him—from whom he hung out with to his work history. In looking into his work history, I discovered that he had made an insurance claim for a workplace accident, in which he had lost his right forefinger. It was my "Aha!" moment. I had all of the bank surveillance photos blown up and, using a magnifying glass, went over the photos pixel by pixel. I discovered exactly what I needed.

During the testimony of FBI agent Dean Steiger, who had worked with me on the case, I asked whether he could show the jury the photo enlargements from the surveillance cameras. I then asked him to tell the jury how the robber held the gun. "The assailant did not hold the gun with his trigger finger," he said, pointing it out on our poster-size blow-ups. "He held it with his middle finger, and there is a flap of skin where the forefinger would be. The assailant is missing his right forefinger."

I turned to the defendant and gave my Perry Mason moment. "Mr. Miller," I said, "will you please show the jury your right hand?"

As a result of doing my homework, nine-fingered John Edward Miller is serving a 104½ year sentence without parole.

The same "do your homework" theory works just as well outside of the courtroom. If, for example, you feel that your oil company has overcharged you for servicing your boiler, you'll be much more prepared to discuss the bill if you've found out what they've charged other people and what other oil companies are charging for the same service. This fact can be found out with a few simple phone calls to neighbors and other oil companies. If you think your property taxes are unusually high, you can find out how much your neighbors are paying and the square footage of their property at your town hall, before making your case to the town tax assessor. If at work, you find that you're getting the short end of the stick when it comes to vacation days, you'd best know the exact differences between what you're getting and what your coworkers are getting for working the same number of years at the company before you go to your boss.

These facts, if they are in your favor, give you an unstoppable advantage.

Before speaking, acting, or reacting to almost everything in life, you need to gather your facts. Every important decision and conversation you've ever had or will have has its own set of facts and evidence. But how do you get the facts that will give you The Truth Advantage? Most of us don't have friends in the FBI or the CIA who can do investigations for us. So, you're thinking you're powerless, right? You're not. Every individual has the opportunity to find facts. You simply have to be smart about where to look and what to ask.

Let me remind you of one of my favorite stories about a woman named Erin Brockovich. Even though she lacked a formal education and had no money, she single-handedly put together a case that resulted in a $333 million settlement, the largest ever paid in a direct-action lawsuit in the United States. How'd she do it? She did her homework and followed one fact to another.

After stumbling on some interesting medical records at the law office where she was clerking, she decided to talk to the family these belonged to. They were being asked, *coerced* might be a better word, to sell their property to the local power company. In talking to them, she learned that chromium was in their groundwater and a series of strange illnesses had occurred in the family. She visited a university chemistry lab to find out the properties of chromium, a rust inhibitor in power plants. She learned that chromium 6 is highly carcinogenic.

She consulted the county water board and collected records of well tests that proved the existence of chromium 6 in the groundwater. She collected water samples from various sites around town and dead frogs from the runoff. She discovered that the power plant's cooling towers were indeed being kept rust-free by chromium and that the plant was dumping its excess water into ponds. She looked up local laws and learned that it was mandated that these runoff ponds be lined. They weren't.

She then researched all of the buyouts of the properties by the power company and compiled page after page of medical records documenting the many health issues of the families who lived there. She also traced the path of groundwater from the power company to the contaminated wells. When it came time to present her case, it was a slam dunk.

The facts were clear: the power company knew what it was doing and was covering it up. In short, the power company lied.

Now, your situation doesn't have to be a million-dollar case against a power company. It might be your desire to buy a used car, find a cheaper cell phone plan, work a better position in your company, or find a new job altogether. Or maybe you want to find out more about your family history or develop a better relationship with your kids or partner. Whatever your personal goal with the truth, doing your homework will ease your mind and help you get there.

The first thing that I always do when I approach a case or any situation in my life is ask a lot of questions. I suppose I first learned this from my dad, the FBI agent. I couldn't get away with anything while living in a house with him. He'd hear me getting into the cookie jar in the morning and call out from his bed. "What are you doing?"

"I'm counting the cookies," I'd mumble with my mouth full of cookies.

"What's in your mouth?" he'd ask.

"Nothing."

"Nothing sounds like something." Oops, caught again.

In the afternoons, his car would come down the driveway, and I'd rush to turn off *Gilligan's Island.* He'd come in and feel whether the TV was warm. "Were you really doing your homework?" How could I lie? He had the facts. I was caught, again! No wonder I turned into a skinny, honest bookworm!

Dr. Jeffrey Hancock, a lying and technology expert at Cornell University, recounted, "A prison guard friend once told me something very useful. 'If anything feels weird, it is.' We all need to pay more attention to intuition." Intuition is any mother's best friend.

Now, with my own kids, I find myself asking a lot of questions. I find that as a parent, you generally have to be your own private investigator, but sometimes you can get it wrong. Last year, my high school son came home smelling like smoke, and, as most moms would have, I blew up. Rather than asking a question, I instantly tossed out an accusation: "You've been smoking!" First, the look on his face when I accused him told me everything I need to know. Second, had I simply asked, "Hey, Jacob, why do you smell like smoke?" he would have gotten the chance to explain that after the school band performance, he was putting away the drums and stopped to talk to the kids in the parking lot who indeed were smoking.

Jacob turned the fact-gathering question back on me. "Mom," he said, "You know me. Have I ever done something to make you not trust me?" The honest answer was no, he hadn't. In fact, he had deposited a lot of capital in what I call the "Trust Bank." The same goes for your spouse, your friends, and your colleagues. If they've never given you any reason to doubt them, why doubt them? On the other hand, if they're always letting you down, even with something as seemingly insignificant as "I'll call you tomorrow" (and then there's no call!), they are making withdrawals from the Trust Bank. Follow-through is a "tell" of credibility.

There's an old lawyer joke I love:

Prosecutor: I'll ask you one more time. Did you, sir, shoot Mr. Jones?

Defendant: No, sir, I did not.

Prosecutor: Sir, do you know what the penalty for perjury is?

Defendant: Yes, I do. And it's a lot better than the penalty for murder!

Sometimes people don't want to answer questions. Our kids, for example, don't want to discuss their texts, their chats, or their friends on Myspace and Facebook. A friend recently asked me, "Does anyone really know how to raise a teenager? Or are we supposed to try to live through it and hope that one day they will be productive members of society?" What are good ways to approach a teenager's reticence and get the facts without causing alarm? How do we find out what they are doing, so we can help them appropriately?

Now, here are a few lawyers' tricks to asking questions:

- **Know what you want to achieve.** Many times with our kids, what we want is just to keep them safe and help them find their successful paths in life. We want to protect them from the things that might have negative effects on their well-being and encourage them toward things that are positive. So, The Truth Advantage is to discover and explain how they can lead safer, better lives. At the workplace, the truth we want to convey might be that we deserve a long-overdue raise. At home, the simple truth is that we'd be happier if our partners would help a little more around the house.

- **Remember that getting angry will do you no good.** No matter how belligerent, sarcastic, or uncommunicative someone becomes, don't let it get under your skin. Instead, stay calm. "You're so critical of me," your child or partner might say. Respond with a question such as "You know I want the best for you, right?" or "You know how much I love you, right?"

- **Get the person to agree with you.** Any great attorney will tell you to move your examination along one question at a time. In court, we do "Your name is, your birthday is, your address is . . ." as a way of relaxing the witness and to get him or her to begin answering honestly. In your own life, the same technique is easy to apply. With your kids: "You're a teenager now, right?" "You're going to want to be driving soon?" "Do you want us to keep trusting you?" So, far, we've got yes, yes, and yes. With your boss: "You know how much I love my job?" "You know my sales have increased year after year?" "Did you know my kids are getting older?" One fact at a time. Your boss has agreed yes, yes, and yes. Now, when the questions turn harder, these relatively benign facts will help bolster the ones that will make a difference to your real objective.

- **Present what you know.** With your kids, you have the outrageous phone bill. "Have you been texting in the middle of the night?" "Who have you been texting so much to?" "Your grades have been dropping since you got the cell phone." Then you have your boss, who hasn't let you go on spring break with your kids in three years. "Have you noticed I've been working from weekends on my BlackBerry?" "Does your family ever get to take a vacation together?" "Would you believe me if I told you it would help me become an even better worker if I got to spend some quality time with my kids before they are grown up and gone?"

- **Stack one fact on top of another fact.** All of these facts are now built from the ground up. The person you're talking to has agreed, agreed, and agreed. You're getting somewhere, and you've got facts to stand on.

- **Anticipate their arguments.** Your kids: "Everyone is texting a lot." Yes, but have everyone's grades decreased?

"You're way too strict." What you call strict, I call love and concern. "You're not a good parent." Let's try turning off your phone at a decent hour for a few weeks and see whether your grades improve. Your boss: "We can't spare you." I can get a lot done on my BlackBerry on the road. "You take enough time off." I've always been accommodating to everyone's schedules and haven't ever had a spring break with my children. "It will hurt the company." What will hurt the company is if I miss the important part of being a parent and become the employee no one wants around, because I've been frustrated and sad. Let me have some fun with my kids this once, please.

- **Write your questions down.** If you are not overly confident with your memory or are afraid you'll veer off course, make some notes on the questions you'd like to ask. Reporters do. Lawyers do. You can, too. I've generally found that when someone sees that you've taken the time to think about your questions in advance, he or she takes what you say more seriously and is more interested in helping you.

    When you think through what you want to achieve, asking questions isn't difficult. In fact, it's a formula for true success.

Research isn't only for librarians and journalists. Research can be a great tool for anyone. "Research is formalized curiosity," said Zora Neale Hurston, the author of the *Their Eyes Were Watching God*. "It is poking and prying with a purpose." With the advent of the Internet, anyone can snoop around and find a few answers. That's not to say that everything you read on the Internet is true, but by doing a little digging, you can find out a great deal of information and then cross-check your gathered facts.

Let me give you some examples.

I was recently buying a car, as most of us do. On this occasion, I was buying a used car so that my son would have his own vehicle. The salesman thought he had the sale locked up. We arrived at a price, but when I said I was going to do some research, he protested. "What do you need to do research for? This car is a great car. It has a clean bill of health." He then proceeded to tell me that I was wasting my time looking around and risking the chance that someone would come in and snatch this great deal on the car.

The fact was that I had seen the Carfax commercials, and I knew the taunting promise: "Don't run the risk of buying a used car with hidden problems." I was going to get a detailed vehicle report before I bought my new used car. I told the dealer I'd need a report from the site, and if he wanted the deal, he'd pull it up. He entered the Vehicle Identification Number of the car, and suddenly I had in front of me every oil change that had ever been done, as well as the fact that it had been wrecked. Okay, it was a minor accident, a fender bender, but guess what? Having that fact, I told the dealer the truth: I was surprised that he had failed to mention that the car had been wrecked. I had The Truth Advantage. He immediately offered me $2,000 off the purchase price, and I bought it on the spot.

Let's talk a little more about the Internet. Have you ever forwarded an e-mail, accepting and believing it to be the truth, only to later learn it wasn't true? I find that what makes many of these e-mail chains believable is that they are substantiated by credible sources such as law enforcement personnel, respected businesses, and celebrities. Don't feel bad, we all can fall victim to these schemes. *PC World* magazine recently compiled a list of "The Worst Internet Hoaxes," and topping out at the most ridiculous of them all is what's known as "the Nigerian E-Mail Scam." All of us would love to believe that a wealthy foreigner needs our assistance to move millions of dollars, and that's why many people convince themselves it's true. But it's not. The scam has been around since the 1920s, when it was called "Spanish Prisoner" and was delivered by snail mail post-marked in Nigeria or another foreign country.

We now can take advantage of technology for a lot of research, but we need to be careful about getting multiple sources. If, for example, you receive an e-mail and want to question its validity, Snopes.com is a reference source for urban legends, folklore, myths, rumors, and misinformation. It's pretty easy to use, and before you pass along something that isn't true, visit the site.

Just this week I received an e-mail from a friend. "Pepsi has a new patriotic can coming out," it began, "with pictures of the Empire State Building and the Pledge of Allegiance on them. But Pepsi forgot two little words on the pledge, 'Under God.' Pepsi said they did not want to offend anyone." Then she attested that this was true. I quickly went to Snopes and discovered that this falsity had been circling the globe on the Internet since shortly after the attacks on the World Trade Center, and one version actually said it was Coke. "Neither soda company is producing or has ever produced or designed cans bearing any portion of the Pledge of Allegiance or an image of the Empire State Building." A simple three-minute check could have stopped my friend from forwarding the inaccurate e-mail.

In a few clicks, you'll find out whether what you're passing along is based on fact or rumor. Then, cross-check those facts with another site on the Internet, such as with the Google or Yahoo! search engine. The Internet is a great tool to help you pack a suitcase full of facts on any subject.

What about your kids? How do you get the facts about what they are doing on the Internet? Here are some ideas that have worked for me:

We have the computer in a public place. I can't always watch every time they go to a website, but when my thirteen-year-old daughter is on the computer in our family room, the fact is I'm a little more sure that she's not doing something scary. Second, I always ask to see my kids' personal websites. I want to know what they are doing on the Web, particularly what personal things they are sharing on sites such as Myspace and Facebook. That's how I found out that our address was listed for the world to see! Third, I get my kids to help me with my own sites and my Tweets. This lets them know that the same rules apply for me. They can see the facts I'm sharing with the world, and I can see the facts they are sharing with the world. Finally, check the "history" of the websites they've been on. That'll show you pretty quickly if there's something you need to discuss with them.

The same is true of your relationships, with both friends and spouses. If you want to find out something about someone or something, start digging around on the Internet. Both it and the computer leave a trail of cookie crumbs.

"It's easier to lie with technology," Dr. Hancock told me, "but it's also easier to get caught. Digital things are highly recordable."

What we do on the Internet is so trackable that a new survey by the American Academy of Matrimonial Lawyers says that two-thirds of divorce lawyers are now using Facebook as the "primary source" of evidence in divorce proceedings. According to the *Guardian*, the site is "a leading cause of relationship trouble." Tip for cheaters: Consider it a billboard to the world! If you post something on the Internet, it will be seen by an infinite number of eyeballs in perpetuity. And if you send an e-mail, it's not going away. There will always be a record of it somewhere. If someone really wants to find it, they will.

---

TRUTH ADVANTAGE DO'S AND DON'TS!

DO always triple-check your facts with two or three good
    sources.
DON'T rely on rumor, gossip, or innuendo as fact.

---

Here's the bottom line on gathering facts: the more you know. the better. If you're buying a house, you get a building inspection. Why? You want to know the truth! How long is the roof going to last? When is the boiler going to die? Are there any traces of termites? When you know these things, you'll have The Truth Advantage on the price. If you're getting a job, you want to know what the national average of someone in that field makes. (There's a website for that: payscale.com.) Why? You'll know what to ask for when the potential employer asks, "What are your salary requirements?" If you're hiring a baby-sitter for your children, you ask for references. Why? You want your children to be safe.

On TV, I can be wrong on my opinion, but I can't be wrong on my facts. Once you get the facts, it is then up to you how to deal with them. Think of each fact as being like a dot on a children's Connect the Dot drawing. When you start connecting them, the full picture begins to take shape. Make sure your picture is detailed, fair, and accurate.

Now it's time to think about all of this.

---

## THE TRUTH ADVANTAGE CHECKUP
### *Just Give Me the Facts, Please*

**Investigating isn't only for detectives.**
- Realize that the more you know, the better you are prepared.
- Take time to do your homework.
- Know that whether you think your husband is cheating or you're being underpaid at work, the importance of getting the complete picture can't be overstated.

**Know the difference.**
- Realize that just because something sounds like a fact (or you want it to be!) doesn't make it so.
- Take time to question your thinking and make sure to triple-check your objectivity.
- Know that if you assume, it can make an "ass of 'u' and me."

**The more you know, the better.**

- Realize that laziness does not give you The Truth Advantage.
- Make an extra effort to get as much information as you can. It will make a difference between your winning and losing.
- Know that the more you find out, the stronger you can make your case.

CHAPTER 9

# Key 4: Think before You Speak

*Think twice before you speak once.*

—ENGLISH PROVERB

"Thank God for dead soldiers." "Thank God for 9/11." "God Hates Fags." These are just a few of the abhorrent signs and verbal attacks being made on a regular basis by members of the Westboro Baptist Church. The Topeka, Kansas, church, which is made up of Pastor Fred Phelps and his family (including two daughters and four grandchildren), has been controversial for years. Jews, gays, Catholics, Muslims, and Hindus are just a few of the groups that the Westboro Baptist Church hates. The church also hates Christians because, according to its views, Christians "have created an atmosphere in this world where people believe the lie that God loves everybody." In short, they are a hate group, spewing their venom at every opportunity.

One way that the Phelps family pushes their hate is by picketing near the funerals of American soldiers killed in combat in Iraq or Afghanistan. In March 2006, the family picketed near the funeral of U.S. Marine Lance Corporal Matthew A. Snyder, who had been killed in Iraq. As a family attempted to bury their heroic son in a peaceful ceremony, the Phelps family chanted derogatory slurs and held their neon signs of hate in the air.

What came afterward was a legal battle that worked its way up to the Supreme Court in a case called *Snyder v. Phelps*. Albert Snyder, Matthew Snyder's father, had sued the Phelpses for invasion of privacy and intentional infliction of emotional distress. A federal jury of his peers, people like you and me, awarded Snyder $11 million in damages. A Court of Appeals later overturned that decision and even ordered Snyder to pay Fred Phelps's legal fees! The decision was appealed to the U.S. Supreme Court. Finally, in March 2011, the Supreme Court, the court of last resort, ruled in favor of Phelps on grounds of the First Amendment. Despite the distress that the Phelpses caused to Snyder's family, the Supreme Court's 8–1 decision was that the Westboro Baptist Church had every legal right to congregate and speak out.

I think the Supreme Court got it wrong. As the sole dissenting justice, Samuel Alito wrote that the First Amendment should be honored, but "it does not follow, however, that they may intentionally inflict emotional injury on private persons at a time of intense emotional sensitivity by launching vicious verbal attacks that make no contribution to public debate."

In his nightly "Talking Points Memo," Bill O'Reilly said, "The bad guys won." And I agreed. I maintain that we must not stifle public debate and that free speech must be protected, but the time, place, manner restriction should have been applied. You can't yell "Fire!" in a crowded theater unless there is really cause for alarm. Why? Those words are intended to cause immediate panic, and people could be harmed as they stampede toward the theater exits.

The Supreme Court could have relied on what is known as the "Fighting Words" doctrine, established in the 1942 ruling *Chaplinsky v. New Hampshire.* "Fighting words" were defined as words that, by their very utterance, inflict injury or tend to incite an immediate breach of the peace. To me, it seems as if the Westboro Baptist Church could be the poster child for this.

The Westboro Baptist Church represents the ultimate power and freedom granted to us by the First Amendment. Yet sadly, it also represents some of the worst human qualities and how off course some people are in preaching their message. We all have a right to share our true feelings, but there is a time, a place, and an appropriate way to do so. Bullying will never be the way to establish communication or understanding.

Just because we are granted the right to speak out, that doesn't mean there isn't a wrong way to do so. What the Phelps family doesn't understand is that insults, harassment, and fear-mongering will never make anyone listen to them. In fact, their techniques drive people away. The Phelpses are certainly not the first group of people to spew racism or homophobia, but their extremist, terrorist tactics only make people view them as villains. The sad irony is that the Phelpses believe that they are acting as messengers of God. When you say something that is intended to harm, you can't get much more depraved than that.

"I've finally learned in life that not everyone is nice," Joslyn, a thirty-one-year-old in Missouri, wrote. "You have to learn to ignore a lot of people who don't want anyone to be happy." Let's face it, the old saying "sticks and stones will break my bones, but words will never hurt me," is absurd poppycock. The Westboro Church is a case in point. While heartbroken families just want to peacefully bury their sons and daughters who died in battle while serving their country, they are forced to listen to these "fighting words." Not that I want to be hit with sticks and stones, but a bruise eventually goes away, while an insult is forever.

The Westboro Baptist Church does lead by example—of what not to do. When you're trying to convince someone of a principle, an idea, or a precept, assaulting him with words will never get you anywhere (except perhaps on his bad side). In fact, by insulting someone, you are slamming the door on any possibility of communication. In your relations with others, keep the Westboro Baptist Church in mind, because it will remind you that no one wants to pet a snarling dog. Insults or questioning someone's morality have exactly the same effect. They only make the insulted person want to run the other way or turn on you and fight.

I'm reminded of a good rule of thumb a law school professor once told me about word choice, "If you wouldn't write it and sign it, you shouldn't say it." When you are thinking about what you might say to someone or about someone, ask yourself this: If I were to be quoted in the newspaper, could I live with having said it? And furthermore, will my words help me convince others of the truth I want to convey?

Have you ever wished your mouth had a rewind or delete key? I know I have. Sometimes we say something to a person in the heat of the moment without giving it much thought or even thinking that it will help our case. Remember this: it won't, and it doesn't.

I've been sparring with Bill O'Reilly for the last ten years at Fox News Channel, but how I got there is a tale of knowing to think before I speak. It was about making the decision to truthfully speak my opinion, but doing so in a way that continued the conversation, rather than ended it.

At the time when I met Bill, I was living in Seattle, working at a big law firm, and teaching law at the University of Washington. At six feet four, Bill can be intimidating, but we launched into a debate about the talking point of the day: Gary Condit, the congressman from California, was involved in a scandal. Condit had lied about an affair with his intern Chandra Levy, and she was now missing and presumably dead. Bill's position was that the congressman should resign.

What I thought was, "You're wrong!" But what I said was, "I can see why you'd think that, and if you were a voter in California, you could make that decision. He's their congressman, and if they don't want him serving, they'll vote him out." My legal training helped me disagree, yet converse with one of the most skilled debaters in the news business. Within two minutes, we were in a heated conversation, and his office had filled with a crowd of producers and staff. When I reminded him that our justice system had been built on the concept of innocent until proven guilty, Bill retorted, "But he lied!" Fox News Channel offered me a job. Sticking to the truth, my truth, got me that job.

What I have learned in the courtroom is that it is possible to disagree with someone and take the opposing side, without demonizing the person. After all, there are two differing sides in every court case. There is, of course, disagreement, but there's an art to disagreement. It is possible to question an opinion without insulting someone or being rude, and it can be done with a smile on your face.

I know what you're probably thinking: if you disagree with something or someone, why should you have to watch your tongue? Why not just "tell it like it is" or go in with bullhorn blaring? Because such a course of action generally gets you nowhere.

Perhaps you remember when South Carolina congressman Joe Wilson yelled, "You lie!" to President Obama in front of a joint session of Congress? Perhaps he should have thought through his actions and remembered Proverbs 17:28, which says, "Even a fool, when he holds his peace, is counted wise: and he that shuts his lips is esteemed a man of understanding." Though Wilson apologized, his harsh words were already spoken. According to "Jefferson's Manual," Thomas Jefferson's guideposts for House operations, House members may not call the president a "liar" or accuse him of "lying" on the House floor. Ideas may be booed, as the Democrats did to President Bush, but to suggest that a president is a liar is unacceptable. Majority Whip Jim Clyburn made the point that "to heckle is bad enough, but to use that word—the one three-letter word that was not allowed in my house when I was growing up—is beyond the pale."

Margaret Paul, a psychologist and a relationship expert, told me, "It is never healthy to attack or judge another under the guise of 'I'm just being honest.' My client's husband said to her, 'I'm just being honest—you disgust me.' You can't be more unhealthy, hurtful, and blaming." Even though she may forgive, it's hard to forget that sting.

There is infinite power in words, and we must cautiously select and use them because once they've been spoken, they can't be sucked back into the mouth. Our words often get us in trouble. Why? Once spoken aloud, they can cause harm or make us look foolish. Or as Mark Twain put it, "It is better to keep your mouth closed and let people think you are a fool than to open it and remove all doubt."

It is much wiser to do what many mothers have told their children, "When you're angry, count to ten before you say anything." Or at least think twice. Rob, a thirty-eight-year-old in Virginia, recounted a childhood lesson in his comments on the American Truth Survey, "My mother always said that if I ever called someone a liar, I'd get my mouth washed out with soap. The day I found out about Santa, I called her a liar. And got my mouth washed out with soap." The practice of "thinking before you speak" in any relationship helps ensure that you don't say something you'll regret (or get your mouth washed out with soap!).

---

TRUTH ADVANTAGE DO'S AND DON'TS!

**DO** ask yourself, "Would I write this in a letter?"
**DON'T** catch "foot in mouth" disease by speaking from anger.

---

Taking a "time-out" is the verbal equivalent of the "Brady Law," the forty-eight-hour period of time you wait after applying for a handgun. It's a mandatory "cooling off period," in an effort to prevent someone from doing something he might later regret. A time-out gives you a moment to ask yourself whether you should say anything at all, and then, if you decide to say something, to thoughtfully consider an appropriate response. Sometimes you'll decide it is indeed better to walk away, rather than toss out heated words in the moment, even though the words may be exactly what you feel.

A smart person, one who wants to have his truth heard and accepted, is someone who thinks before putting his mouth in drive. I remember once reading Ann Lander's advice column, in which she shared the thought that "the trouble with talking too fast is you may say something you haven't thought of yet." That can quickly lead to "foot in mouth disease." Sometimes silence is golden. It gives you a moment to catch your thoughts before they trap you. And if someone is trying to lure you into a fight, here's a tip I've taught my law students: think of a fish. It will be a whole lot better off if it keeps its mouth shut and examines the situation before opening it and getting hooked.

If you've thought through something—given consideration to the weight of what you're saying—you generally achieve positive results. I learned this in the high-stakes environment of the courtroom, and I've used it to survive the high-pressure environment of TV news. I know that whatever comes out of my mouth can and will be used against me. Most of the things I regret saying in my life were said in the heat of the moment, in situations where I was upset, angry, or hurt. I vividly recall moments in which I have been uncharacteristically sharp. I've fired off an angry e-mail and only after hitting SEND did I think about the ramifications. I've told the customer service person at my cable company that her "service stinks, and your company should be out of business." In each instance, the utterance only pushed me backward in dealing with that person, not forward. The person who received the e-mail was enraged. The cable company didn't give me better service. Although in neither instance will I ever have face-to-face interactions with those people, I still think of both incidents often and realize that my actions and reactions could have been better. I didn't feel good about it, and I know it did neither party any good. I've since learned that if my inclination is to send an angry e-mail, I should write it, save it in my drafts folder, and look at it again the next day. Most of the time, I discover that it needs a complete rewrite. And in dealing with customer service people, I have realized that killing them with kindness gets me a lot faster service.

Yet the situation grows worse when the person you insult is close to you or works with you, and you have to continue to deal with him or her on a daily basis. It's hard to take a breath. It's easier to say, "You bozo." This last summer, I was furiously typing up my notes to a producer for a show that night, and my law intern came into my office and asked, "What do you think about war?" I lost track of what I was writing, and I was on a major deadline. He obviously didn't realize he was intruding, but I was so mad I wanted to spit. "I don't like war," I said, trying to find the good spot in my heart. Then I growled, "But how about we talk about it later?" After my show that night, I took him aside and kindly explained that when I'm on fire getting ready for a show, I can't be discussing philosophical questions of the ages. Yet every time I look at him, I still think about the time I growled.

A few years ago, when we first moved into our new house, I wanted to give my daughter a special birthday gift. I had her room decorated and excitedly picked out some fabrics with a decorator for her window dressings, with a matching tufted headboard and pillows. The fabrics were late coming in, and the designer got delayed, and finally, way after her birthday, the day came for the installation. It was a disaster. We excitedly watched as the installation was done, and everything was the wrong size—from the window dressing to the headboard. The designer said he'd fix it but wanted me to pay the balance of the bill for which I had already paid a generous deposit, and to add insult to injury, he wanted to charge me for the additional fabric. So I did what any mom might have done, I lost it! That guy didn't know what hit him, and I am not proud to say I did this in front of my daughter. Even though her room does look lovely, when he came back for the last install, he asked if I had any other projects in mind. I said, "Yes. But not with you!" I was still a little nasty. I just couldn't get over it. And my punishment? Every time I look at the room, instead of seeing how pretty it is, I think about how nasty I got.

It's okay to have the thoughts. It's human nature. But as any good carpenter (or decorator!) will tell you, in your words and deeds, you are better served by measuring twice, cutting once.

If you're like me, you want those occasions to be rare. None of us wants to be the person who erupts in anger at the slightest provocation, the type whose words are like a machete cutting through life, ready to take down anyone in his way. Have you ever been at a restaurant with someone who is downright nasty to the server? Remember how it made you feel bad for the server, but worse at the thought of what might become of your food in the kitchen? Our chosen words paint a portrait of who we are as people. There's nothing worse than watching someone go down in flames because the words that person has chosen have popped a hole in his or her balloon. Approaching others with kindness will keep you from regretting what you said or did. It will certainly make others more receptive to your thoughts and more apt to help you get what you want.

English poet William Blake had the right idea when he said, "A truth that's told with bad intent is worse than all the lies you can invent." The truth is not vindictive. Honesty is not to be used as a sword. We shouldn't use knowledge of someone's flaws or weaknesses as an opportunity to injure the person, and doing so certainly won't help you sway him or her to your way of thinking. Even when your truthful message may be hard for someone to hear, you should not intend to hurt that person when you share it. In speaking honestly, we don't want to be offensive or to arouse resentment. We want to present the truth from a good place. As my grandmother always said (and yours might have, too): "You can catch more flies with honey than vinegar."

Yes, words communicate how we feel, but in delivering them, we must also think about how they are going to make the other person feel. Words have the power to unite or divide, and if you choose your words carefully and kindly, you are more likely to get someone to see your way of thinking.

Relationship expert Margaret Paul says, "There are only two possible intents: to protect against pain/loss with some form of controlling behavior, or to learn about loving yourself and others. When people choose the intent to protect/control, they come from the ego wounded part of themselves and are only intent on gaining control or not being controlled. When people choose the intent to learn/love, this is the intent that is necessary for relationships to thrive—whether they are personal, business, political, or global."

I've studied jurors in the courtroom. I've watched how they respond to hostile witnesses. They don't like them. I've watched how they respond to attorneys who froth at the mouth. They *really* don't like them. And then I've watched how jurors respond when something is presented to them honestly, openly, and kindly. They like it, and they listen. In the end, attitude drives their decision making. Jurors are like trees—if they are leaning one way, they'll usually fall that way. When I'm advocating in court, I know that my words will help them either lean toward me or lean away from me.

Certainly, there will be times of dogged disagreement in a courtroom. Similarly, on both sides of the political aisle, on both sides of the desk, on both sides of the bed, there is one thing that we must remember: What we say is more than "just words." Words have infinite power. Words matter. Words can carry a punch stronger than any physical blow. In his Abraham Lincoln's first inaugural address, he told our country, "We are not enemies, but friends. We must not be enemies."

Yoko Ono once said, "Your words will run around forever to reverberate in the ocean of the world like a pebble you dropped in the water. Let's believe in that power—the larger power that could move the mountain and the ocean." Agreed.

Here's something I've often experienced in the courtroom: An unscrupulous (in my mind) defense attorney will say something to a witness that is totally outrageous and absolutely not true. For example, "Isn't it true, sir, that you beat your wife?" Of course, like any good opposing counsel, I would stand up quickly and say, "Objection!" His statement is made up of empty air and is very prejudicial to my case. Even though the judge will sustain the objection, strike the question from the record, and instruct the jury to disregard the question, the damage has already been done. You can't unring the bell. The jury has already heard the titillating question and then had it underlined by the judge. Even though it has no basis in truth, it has already been spoken and heard. It suddenly becomes the elephant in the room. The jury wonders, "What would have been the answer to that question?"

The same is true with the things we say. Even though we may retract them, apologize, or say we misspoke, the words are already out there. They've been said and will ripple about with unknown consequences.

I recently heard a newlywed wife joke to her spouse, "I would have married you for your life insurance alone." What does that mean? Even though she was kidding, everyone who heard her say it certainly questioned her sincerity. And we can assume that it planted a seed of doubt about their relationship that might come back to haunt both her and her husband.

We all get angry sometimes and say hurtful things, but there are some things that should never come out of your mouth. A good friend often reminds me, "Don't ever say something to someone that, to them, is the most hurtful thing they could ever hear." To a spouse: "I wish I never married you." To your kids: "I wish I never had you." To your boss: "You're an idiot!" Those words will only create a deep cut that might never heal. Those thoughts are hard to recover from, not because you can't sincerely apologize for them (words such as these probably evoke the most sincere of apologies), but they breed doubt and resentment that will not be easy for the person to ever forget. Even if that person says he or she forgives you, you might never forgive yourself for hurting the individual in such a way.

If you don't throw a stone, the water won't ripple.

I recently passed a sign outside a restaurant that said, "Fresh fish today!" That simple word *today* told me everything I needed to know. It might just be one word, but, boy, it changes your perspective, doesn't it? Or, as Mark Twain put it, "The difference between the right word and the almost right word, is the difference between lightning and the lightning bug."

Thinking before you speak does not mean that you overanalyze and critique everything that comes out of your mouth. Certainly, no one wants every word to be that planned or calculated. After all, as communication professor Dr. Mark L. Knapp said to me, "At some point, people have to accept the world as a complex and imperfect place and that guidelines are just that—guidelines, not edicts."

Thinking before you speak is knowing that words can be heavy hitting and word choice can be crucial in making your life better. The difference between the right word and the almost right word can be the difference between your being denied and rejected and your being respected and well received. If you choose your words well, you'll never have to eat them.

I realize the idea of speaking more "politically correctly" has been discussed ad nauseam. I think it's simple to remember that people are sensitive. I'd be willing to bet you have a hot button—something that makes the hair stand up on the back of your neck—and you'd rather people not push it. People quickly size you up on how you interact with them. Are your words kind or not?

You never want to deliver such a message that the person on the receiving end hears: "I'm smart, you're stupid" "I'm right. You're wrong." "I'm good. You're bad." Instead, you want the person to hear that you're someone who wants to work to make things better. You want to do everything you can to make sure that those words are coming from the right place. You're a stand-up friend, a go-to employee, and a good parent. You're someone who is looking to make conditions in life better, not worse. Again, that is not to say you can't disagree with someone or dislike something. You certainly can, but it always works well to suggest a way to make it better. My approach is to say it the way I'd want to hear it myself.

In addition, whenever I am faced with a situation where I don't like something or am bothered by something, I try to think through to the solution to the problem before I talk with someone about it. Simply put, it's fine to say, "The basement is flooding," but it's more effective to say, "Help me plug in the sump pump!" The same applies to your business and personal life. If you have to tell a friend you're canceling your lunch, break the news to her with a few new dates you have available. If you've got an issue at work, offer the solution to the problem. For example, "I need to be at my daughter's parent/teacher conference Friday morning, but I could do the meeting Friday afternoon easily." I recently had a situation where the production team at Fox had designed the graphic for my show *Wiehl of Justice.* The truth was that I didn't like it. Rather than simply saying, "It doesn't work," I instead said that I liked the color choices they had made, but I had a few ideas about the look of it. Because I didn't insult their work and I offered what I liked about it, along with my idea to make it better, the team enthusiastically helped create a new graphic that looks great.

Adjusting the way that you position something also works with loved ones. Just remember, every snipe and swipe you take and every dig you make will probably come back at some point to haunt you. You may be reminded of it directly, or worse, it may just quietly build resentment. When you say, "You never loved me," or "You never really cared," or "It's always all about you," instead of addressing specific grievances that can be worked on, you are doing yourself and your relationship a disservice.

So, then, how do you disagree or give your honest opinion without being offensive? If you think about it first, there's always a relatively easy fix. Instead of saying, "You don't love me anymore," flip it and try something like, "You used to kiss me in the elevator when no one was looking. Now you don't, and that makes me sad." That'll probably get you kissed in the elevator at least once.

Let's get real. Mistakes happen. Or as Britney Spears sings, "Oops. I did it again." No matter how much we try to count to ten or keep our mouths shut, we are sometimes insulting, rude, or too blunt, particularly with those we're the closest to. We hurt people's feelings, and they tell us so, either by their words or in their actions. You've probably experienced this once or twice in your life. It's called the cold shoulder, or worse, "you're sleeping on the couch."

When you do say something offensive, when you make a misstep, what can you do to fix it? Cara, a forty-four-year-old in Georgia, admitted in her Truth Survey answers that "Sometimes all I want is for my husband to just say he's sorry and give me a hug."

These six steps to a quick resolution will be best received:

1. **Act swiftly.** As soon as you know you've caused offense, take action immediately. This isn't a time to wait it out or throw down the gauntlet and start a stand-off.

2. **Keep it simple.** There's a rule in the courtroom: the less you say, the better off you are in a disagreement. Don't try to overexplain, overanalyze, or do it over. It won't work.

3. **Avoid déjà vu.** Don't say, "I didn't mean to hurt your feelings," or, "That shouldn't upset you." The obvious responses from the offended party are "Then why did you say what you said?" and "But it does." Instead try, "I should have been more thoughtful."

4. **Listen.** Communication is key in any relationship. If the person you've offended wants to talk about it more, be all ears. Cutting him or her off or saying, "Let's move on," will incite more anger.

5. **Apologize again.** Do so sincerely, with a smile, a hug, or a kiss, as appropriate.

6. **Celebrate.** Be happy that you have survived and been forgiven for one of your foibles, and promise that you'll try harder next time.

Next, let's figure out your timing!

---

## THE TRUTH ADVANTAGE CHECKUP
### Mind First, Mouth Second

**Don't be a bully.**

• Realize that no one responds well to insults, hurtful remarks, or obscenity.

• Know that it is possible to communicate effectively without terrifying someone.

• Take note that people respond better to a dog that isn't barking.

**Imagine yourself being quoted.**

• Ask yourself, would you be okay with everyone knowing what you said?

• Don't write anything online that you don't want the whole world to see. It follows you everywhere.

• Know that if you are going to regret saying something after it's been said, you shouldn't let the words ever spill out of your mouth.

• If you imagine what other people would think of you if they heard you talking, this is a good way to keep yourself in line.

**Don't ever say the worst possible thing to someone.**

• Realize that everyone has a raw nerve, a sensitive spot.

• Think about the people you're close to, and make note of what the worst possible thing is for them.

• Never go there—not even when you are angry, hurt, or upset. You won't be able to take it back.

CHAPTER 10

# Key 5: Time It Right

*A stone thrown at the right time is better than gold*
*given at the wrong time.*

—PERSIAN PROVERB

"Goddamn America!" and "America's chickens are coming home to roost." You might remember the harsh
words of aspiring presidential candidate Barack Obama's
pastor and mentor Reverend Jeremiah Wright, who shortly
after 9/11 had made scandalous remarks about America and
its future. In 2008, during the frenzy of election-year politics,
these words came back to haunt Mr. Obama. By mid-March,
Obama was in a neck-and-neck battle to become the Demo-
cratic candidate, but he had a growing scandal on his hands
that had the potential to squash his candidacy. Many of Reverend Wright's comments were available on DVD, were
being circulated by the media, and were headlining the
news cycle.

How would Obama handle the situation? Everyone was wondering whether he thought Wright was wrong. If this was Obama's mentor, how could he reconcile such inflammatory statements? And when would he finally address the controversy, which was at a fevered pitch and growing louder every day?

Finally, a few weeks after the story first broke, Obama took the initiative to deliver his now legendary speech on race: "A More Perfect Union." He addressed the situation head on, dealing with the anger and frustration of centuries of troubled race relations and offering a vision of how to surmount those problems. He picked the perfect time and had people hanging on his every word.

"We've heard," he said to the crowd gathered around him in Philadelphia and to millions more sitting around their radios, TVs, and computers, "my former pastor, Reverend Jeremiah Wright, use incendiary language to express views that have the potential not only to widen the racial divide, but views that denigrate both the greatness and goodness of our nation: that rightly offend white and black alike."

Then Obama took the time to answer and address the painful questions in a full and truthful way: "Did I know him to be an occasionally fierce critic of American domestic and foreign policy? Of course. Did I ever hear him make remarks that could be considered controversial while I sat in church? Yes." His audience was rapt. They realized that the candidate Barack Obama was dealing with an issue that could make or break his campaign. He was compelling.

"Reverend Wright's comments were not only wrong but divisive," Obama said. "Divisive at a time when we need unity, racially charged at a time when we need to come together to solve a set of monumental problems—two wars, a terrorist threat, a failing economy, a chronic health-care crisis, and potentially devastating climate change problems that are neither black or white or Latino or Asian, but rather problems that confront us all."

In short, Barack Obama had The Truth Advantage.

Instead of hurting him, the timing of this speech put wind behind his sails, which he rode all the way to victory. Whether you're a lifelong Democrat, a staunch Republican, or fiercely Independent, you can see that Obama's speech proved that timing it right can foster a "we're in this together" feeling to help ensure that your message is well received.

My friend lives on a road in farm country. While I was visiting him this spring, a local farmer stopped at the top of my friend's driveway to make an adjustment on his tractor. We started talking, and he told us that today was the day to set his strawberry plants. "Why today?" I asked.

"The *Farmers' Almanac* says so," he said. "Today is an extra good day to set strawberry plants." I laughed and then realized he was serious.

"What's next?" I asked.

"Oh," he told me. "Tomorrow is a poor planting day. Tomorrow's the day to break ground."

I later did a little research on the *Farmers' Almanac* and discovered that farmers and gardeners have been using its wisdom since 1818. If there's anyone whose livelihood depends on good timing, it's farmers. If you want to make anything grow well, good timing is key.

Farming is not the only thing that benefits from good timing. Get into a serious conversation with any chef about cooking, and he'll tell you it has a lot to do with timing. If the mashed potatoes and the green beans are ready and the pot roast isn't, the meal is ruined. Ask any comedian: what's the hardest thing about delivering a punch line that leaves people roaring in laughter? It's all about the right timing. An appropriate pause can make a joke; an inappropriate pause can kill a joke. Ask any bird. If the bird could talk, it would tell you that the timing of its migration can be the difference between life and death.

As Ecclesiastes 3:1 says, "There is a right time for everything." It's not just what we say and how we say it that's important. It's also *when* we say it. Presented at an inappropriate time, the truth can fall flat and may put the recipient on the defensive. Knowing there's a right time and a wrong time to present the truth will make it more likely that what you have to say will be received well and have positive results.

What I've realized with my children is that if I have serious issues to discuss with them, I need to find a time when they are most likely to be receptive. With my Dani and Jacob, I've noticed that it's when we're doing something away from the house, perhaps on a bike ride in the park or having ice cream after a ballgame. I've learned that the wrong time is as soon as they get home from school. The same principle applies if we switch roles, and they want to choose the right time to talk to me. In fact, I've told my kids to let me get into my "play" clothes after I get home from work so that I have some transition time before they jump on me with anything really important. My mom has always made a point not to have important conversations with my dad in the car because she noticed that he feels trapped and isn't receptive to her ideas. My friend says some of the best conversations he has with his partner are in the car, because there are no outside distractions and thoughts of work are not consuming them.

The bottom line: if you can create an appropriate environment, you'll give yourself a big head start in promoting positive understanding with another person.

Noted senator George McGovern once joked, "When they say you are ahead of your time, it's just a polite way of saying you have a real bad sense of timing." Yet what is bad timing? And how do you avoid it?

Well, you know it's a bad time if:

- **You're tired.** This seems so simple, but boy, it's crucial. Just as you shouldn't go grocery shopping when you're starving, don't start an important conversation when you're tired. When you're exhausted, there's no way you're going to be able to properly gather your thoughts and express them well. On the flip side, if your listener is exhausted, this person will not give the conversation the attention it deserves, and he or she won't effectively absorb what you're saying. And, heaven forbid that you yawn while someone is telling you something important. It silently screams disrespect. I once knew a judge who would throw anyone who yawned out of his courtroom.

- **You're pressed for time.** Never have an important conversation when you're in a hurry. If you have something you really need to talk about, set aside a time when no one will be rushed. Also, if you only have fifteen minutes, say so at the beginning of the conversation, and make it clear that if you aren't able to finish the conversation, you're prepared to finish it at another time. There's nothing more upsetting than spilling your guts and watching the other person check his or her watch every minute. When you're involved in a serious conversation with someone, having the person's undivided attention is vital to a happy exchange of ideas.

- **You're out with friends.** This should be common sense, but unfortunately, too many times, I've sat with a group around a dinner table and watched as a couple began to have a serious conversation or negotiation about something that was important in their relationship. If you do this, it makes everyone around you feel ill at ease and trapped in your couples' therapy session. Furthermore, when you conduct your discussions in front of others, it's as if you are asking them to take sides, and that puts people in a very uncomfortable position. Your intimate discussions with your partner, colleagues, or children should be carried out at a time when each party can feel comfortable and stay focused. These conversations should be done in a private place where people can openly communicate what's truly on their minds.

- **You're already in an argument.** Don't add fuel to an already-in-progress argument by bringing up another conversation you've been meaning to have. If the argument is about who is taking out the trash, this is not the time to have the "My mother's coming to stay for a week" talk. When the temperature of a conversation is already hot, adding more drama will only make it boil. The best thing to do when you're in an argument is to get over that specific argument before moving on to another one. Creating a new concern will only add more angst and give you less chance of achieving a positive outcome.

- **You're already stressed.** When you're stressed or under pressure, it doesn't allow you to be receptive to others' ideas or to clearly present your own. The energy you need for an important conversation is not available, because it is being consumed by something else. If your partner, for example, has a big project due at work tomorrow morning, tonight is probably not the best time to discuss marital issues. While your children are studying for an exam is not the time to talk about their bad grades. If you attempt to have a serious conversation when you're stressed, stress becomes the lens through which you see the world. It is impossible to cultivate a positive attitude when you are stuck in survival mode. Your focus has to be on putting out the current fire, not on starting and fueling a new one.

I remember a story John F. Kennedy once told about a man who asked his gardener to plant a tree. The gardener responded that it was not a good idea, because the tree was slow growing and would not reach maturity for a hundred years. "In that case," the man said, "there is no time to waste: plant it this afternoon."

When you want The Truth Advantage, you want to have time on your side. When you give thoughtful consideration to the best time to present your ideas, you're giving your desires a leg up.

Celebrities and their publicists know all about the importance of good timing. Most of the time, nothing they say or do is spontaneous; instead, everything is carefully planned to achieve the best kind of attention at the right time. "The Queen of All Media" herself, Oprah Winfrey, is no exception. In late January 2011, Oprah declared that she wanted to share a "bombshell family secret" that she had been unaware of her entire life but that had been revealed to her the previous October. As it turned out, it was a personal, touching discovery: in addition to her two deceased siblings, Oprah had a half-sister named Patricia whom she had never known about.

When Patricia appeared on Oprah's show, it was without a doubt a beautiful family moment. Yet many people began to wonder: if Oprah had learned of her half-sister back in October, why had she waited until January to make the news public? Could this be a well-timed publicity stunt?

A powerful woman such as Oprah Winfrey doesn't need to beg for publicity, but she certainly wanted the ratings for her latest endeavor—her new network, OWN. Revealing her family "miracle" to coincide with the launch of her network was a strategic move that was all about good timing.

Yet good timing isn't only for celebrities. It can work for you, too. From your workplace decisions to dealing with the intricacies of family life, ask yourself when might be the best time to present your needs, to better position you to achieve success.

When do you think, for example, is the best time to ask for a raise? Well, human resource managers say that certain times are definitely bad times to make your request. One is rather obvious: don't ask for a raise the week after mass layoffs. When people are getting pink slips, it's usually an indicator that belt tightening is going on within the company. It would be an awkward time to knock on your boss's door and say, "Hey, I know you fired all of those people, but how about giving me a raise?" Similarly, if you have just received a bad performance review or have lost an important client, it's not the time to say, "I think I should be making more money." Instead, that's the time to ask your boss, "How can I do better?" Asking for money at the end of your company's fiscal year would also be a poorly timed request. Why? Your boss is probably figuring out how much he's gone over his budget during the previous year, and it would only pile more angst onto his budgetary woes.

But don't worry, there are also some great times to ask for a raise, more vacation days, or even a better office. If you've just been given more responsibility or a new position within the company, that's the perfect time to say you're excited about the additional duties and are wondering what the added compensation will be. Or, if you've just landed a big deal or helped increase the company's revenue, it presents a window of opportunity to get a piece of the pie. And if you know the company is strapped and is still asking you to take on a heavier workload, maybe that's the perfect time to request a bigger office or more vacation days in lieu of increased compensation.

Now, let's look at what the experts say about the timing of certain life decisions. Why do so many couples get engaged around the holidays? It's a well-timed decision for several reasons. First, it's easy to get the word out. Friends and family are gathered around during the holidays. Next, it adds a memory that will make the holiday always unforgettable. And economically, if a guy is looking to save a few bucks, an engagement ring means you don't have to buy a Christmas present.

According to the website Edmunds.com, you'll get the ultimate best deal on a car the last week of December. Why? That's when dealers are desperate to meet their yearly quota. If you can't hold off on the purchase until December, the last week of any month is also a good time for the same reason: salespeople want to meet their monthly sales goal. That makes it the perfect time to state the advantage you want: "I'd like your best deal!"

Real estate experts say there's a high season for sales as well and a good time to be a buyer and a seller. Sales climb in April, May, and June because of good weather, pretty flowers, tax rebate checks that can be used toward down payments, and the approaching end of the school year, which gives families freedom to move without disrupting children's schedules. These are the times that sellers will have the advantage. If you're a buyer looking for a great deal, however, try the heat of August. Real estate salespeople report the fewest sales at that time of year, because people go on vacation and prepare to start a new school term.

When might be the best time to deal with those annoying customer service calls you have to make? Well, if you want to have a shorter wait time and a better chance of getting your way, the time to call a customer service sales center at your credit card, cell phone, or cable company is not on Monday. Why? That's when they are inundated with the most calls. Instead, if you can wait until Tuesday afternoon or Wednesday, you may encounter a shorter hold time and customer service representatives who are in a good mood. This translates to a greater chance that they will give you what you want.

In all things, look for the right time, and you will have The Truth Advantage.

How do you also find the right time in your personal encounters?

---

TRUTH ADVANTAGE DO'S AND DON'TS!

DO get time on your side.

DON'T add fuel to a burning fire by bringing up another argument when you're already in one.

---

Though it sounds cliché, everyone's time is valuable. When you recognize and respect other people's time and circumstances, you will improve your chances of being heard and getting what you want.

Here's how to plan your life so that the clock works to give you The Truth Advantage:

- **Make the time.** You don't always have the time to have a serious conversation. If you are about to head into a meeting and your husband calls to talk to you about last night's argument, it's okay to say that you can't talk, but make sure that you set a time to talk soon afterward. It's as simple as, "Honey, I love you and really want to discuss this, but can we talk at four o'clock when I'm out of my meeting?" If you just abruptly say, "Can't talk to you right now," or if you wait too long after the request, the other person will get the sense that you are trying to stall or avoid the topic. By agreeing on a set time, you can ensure that both individuals participating in the conversation will be fully attentive and focused.

- **Know your audience.** Just because it's a good time for you to talk doesn't necessarily mean it isn't a bad time for someone else. You don't want your message to get lost. You wouldn't want to send out an important business e-mail on a Friday evening, and you wouldn't want to spring a weighty conversation on someone whose focus is elsewhere or who doesn't have the time or energy to actively participate. Furthermore, everyone is different— some people are most attentive in the early morning, whereas others don't quite get into the groove until later in the day. If you think through the other times you've had successful conversations with certain people— whether your boss or your spouse—you'll recognize the time that best suits them. If you have to discuss concerns that need the person's full attention, ask to talk when you know he or she will be most receptive.

- **Be present.** We all live fast-paced, busy lives. Even when you are willing to have a serious conversation, you proba- bly still have a million other things to think about. But if you've committed yourself to truly communicating with someone, be sure to push out all of the distracting thoughts. Don't start making a mental list of everything you have to do, such as dropping off the dry-cleaning or picking the kids up from school. This only makes you try to rush through the conversation, and the person will be able to tell. If you respond before someone is done speaking, you're not truly paying attention. I've learned this as a prosecutor as well—if I'm speaking to someone and I'm three questions ahead in my mind, I'm not really listening.

- **Catch the person in a good mood.** If you just heard your boss arguing with his wife over the phone, you probably wouldn't want to go in and ask him for a raise. Similarly, asking your spouse to discuss marital concerns when he or she has just had a bad day at work would be a poor decision. Studies have shown that people who are in a pleasant mood are more receptive to ideas and sugges- tions and tend to show more general awareness. I've noticed firsthand that when I'm in a positive mood, I'm also much less critical.

- **Make it sooner, rather than later.** Just as it's bad to spring something on someone, it is just as bad to wait too long to address it. By avoiding an important conversation, you are wasting time that could be used to address an issue and fix it. If the other person doesn't know what's been bothering you, he or she certainly won't do anything to change it. In addition, it's important to express what you need to, but be succinct in your words and don't drag the conversation out. Clear communication is courteous communication.

If you're a good cook, you know when to take the meat off the grill. If you're a good doctor, you know that early diagnosis saves lives. If you're a stockbroker, you know when to sell and when to buy. And if you're going to succeed in dealing with people, you know that the secret of successful communication is time consideration.

Value somebody's time, and you'll have The Truth Advantage. Now, let's figure out how to admit your mistakes.

---

## THE TRUTH ADVANTAGE CHECKUP
### *Everything Has Its Season*

**There will never be a perfect time.**
- Realize that if you wait until the "perfect" moment to get something done, you'll be waiting a long time.
- Be active in making time for something important.
- Know that being judicious in selecting the right time will give you a real advantage.

**Whoa!**
- Finding the right time means not rushing into a conversation that you or the other person may not be ready to have.
- Make sure you work at finding the most appropriate time in order to get the best results.

- If you know a person well enough, you know when it's a good time and when it's a bad time.

**But don't wait forever.**

- Waiting a little while to find the best time for something is ideal.
- Waiting forever means the right opportunity may have passed you by, turned around, and walked right past you again.
- At some point, you just have to seize the moment and do it!

# CHAPTER 11

# Key 6: Admit Your Mistakes

*Confession is good for the soul.*

—SCOTTISH PROVERB

Tiger Woods. His name is now synonymous with scandal and is now known for all of the wrong reasons. After a bizarre car crash in the early morning hours near his home, years of transgressions began to come to light. At the time, besides being a star golfer, Woods was reportedly earning $110 million per year on endorsements of everything from Nike to Gatorade to Cadillac. One by one, as he failed to address the growing scandal, the companies began to drop him. His brand became more and more tarnished the longer he waited to confront the controversy head on. In short, he got stuck in a sandpit. Due to his secrecy and his unwillingness to answer the accusations of adultery, instead of fading away, the story gained momentum and began to bury him. As any public relations expert will tell you, he didn't get out in front of the issue and take control of the story; the story took control of him.

"I think Tiger Woods's fate would have been different if he had been a bit more open and forthcoming from the beginning," Colleen McCarthy, a public relations expert, pointed out. "He didn't necessarily have to disclose all of his demons, but if he'd made a statement along the lines of 'I've made some mistakes or bad judgment calls, and I am working it out with my family. You may hear things about me, but please respect the privacy of my family.' That would have shut a lot of the press's digging down."

Nobel Peace Prize winner and former secretary of state Henry Kissinger said, "Any fact that needs to be disclosed should be put out now or as quickly as possible, because otherwise, the bleeding will not end." Once you start stonewalling the press or, in fact, anyone you are in a relationship with, people will dig and dig until they find something.

The lack of response and the failure to address any issue head on adds credibility to the accusations, rumors, and sources that come out of the woodwork. Tiger Woods's problem was arrogance, a common flaw of many who make mistakes and think they're going to get away with them. Though his personal life might have been no one's business, when he didn't take the lead to nip the problem in the bud, the problem grew into a giant weed that became impossible to kill.

---

### TRUTH ADVANTAGE DO'S AND DON'TS!

When you have to admit wrongdoing, **DO** rip the Band-Aid off!

**DON'T** sit back and think it will go away. It won't.

---

Stalling only makes it worse. Around the same time as Tiger's troubles surfaced, talk-show host David Letterman also had a problem. A CBS producer, Robert Halderman, tried to blackmail Letterman for two million dollars and threatened to disclose details about Letterman's past affairs with women who had worked on the *CBS Late Show*. David Letterman is the one who broke the story. He first apologized to his staff and told them that his wife had been horribly hurt by the news. Then he went on the air and told his national audience, "I'm glad you folks are here tonight, and I'm glad you folks are in such a pleasant mood, because I have a story I'd like to tell you and the home viewers as well." It seemed as if he was setting up one of his comedy bits. "This morning, I did something I've never done in my life. I had to go downtown and testify before a grand jury. . . . I had to tell them all the creepy things I had done." The audience laughed. Then David confessed, "I have had sex with women who worked for me on this show." The audience sat silent.

After the show that night, CBS released a statement that read, "Mr. Letterman addressed the issue during the show's broadcast this evening and we believe his comments speak for themselves." In his first show after news of the sex scandal broke, Letterman appeared for his nightly monologue and told his audience he was desperately trying to save his marriage. "Let me tell you, folks," he admitted, "I've got my work cut out for me." He then said, "If you hurt a person, and it's your responsibility, you try to fix it." He even cracked a few jokes, saying, "I got in the car this morning, and the navigation lady wasn't speaking to me."

Now, the question I'm going to ask you is this: Do you remember the name of David Letterman's wife or the names of any of the women whom he had an affair with? Probably not. But I'd be willing to bet that you recognize the names Elin Nordegren and Rachel Uchitel. David Letterman's handling of his circumstances shows how we are better served by taking the lead with our painful truths, rather than having them sneak up and hijack us.

When Tiger Woods did finally address his scandal, it was too little, too late. He didn't admit to the affairs and instead asked for privacy while he and his family dealt with his "behavior and personal failings behind closed doors." Had he immediately gone on *Oprah* or sat down with Barbara Walters and admitted to having made serious mistakes and said that he was now working on gaining his wife's forgiveness and on overcoming his addictions, I'm betting the entire scenario would have played out differently.

The ABC-TV family drama *Brothers & Sisters* chronicles the lives of a seemingly perfect all-American family. Matriarch Nora Holden (Sally Field) holds her family together as they deal with divorce, infidelity, addiction, politics, and death. In one of her great motherly moments, Nora once said, "Facing the truth is so much easier than all the time and energy it takes to run away from it." Even though the show is fiction, the sentiment is true. Authenticity is good for your health, and it also clears your mind to immediately give you The Truth Advantage. "A web of deceit is hugely energy draining," Dr. Dale Archer told me. "If we have to keep in mind all of the lies we tell, that's a weight in our minds, utilizing valuable energy in our brains. That takes a huge toll on the individual psyche."

A few years back, a friend wrote me a letter to confess and apologize for having intentionally said things about me that were not true, in order to gain a closer friendship with a mutual friend. Her admission of guilt was a surprise to me, in that I had no previous knowledge of her actions. Her actions hadn't directly affected my life as far as I knew, but obviously they had affected hers. Her conscience was burdened by guilt over what she had done.

As it turned out, she was a recovering alcoholic going through the 12-step program. There's a reason that people who are attempting to recover from addictions are encouraged to amend their relationships as part of the healing and growth process. All of the 12-step programs, including Alcoholics Anonymous, Sex Addicts Anonymous, and Overeaters Anonymous, maintain that confession and apology are crucial steps on the road to recovery. To get better, you must deal with the consequences of the pain you have caused others and take responsibility for it. Step 8 of the 12-step program encourages those in recovery to examine their relationships, both past and present, and make a list of the people they have hurt, with the hope that they will make amends for their wrongs. Step 9 involves taking direct action to rectify the damages they've done to the people they've hurt. In taking these steps, participants say their lives blossom, bad relationships are healed, and self-worth is renewed.

I saw that old friend recently at the grocery store. She looked much healthier and seemed much more clear-headed and grounded. We ended up exchanging one of the most sincere hugs in recent memory. Her willingness to take responsibility for having gossiped about me gained my respect and helped revive our friendship. By actively making amends for the past, she was able to move on in her recovery and rid herself of a poison that had been consuming her.

People who keep secrets or feel guilty about their transgressions suffer not only mentally, but physically as well. You know why a lie detector works? It works because our bodies give off clues. When we are being dishonest, our blood pressure and our heart rate both dramatically rise. Lies make us twitch, redden, and perspire.

Body language expert Tonya Reiman explained, "Short of a confession, there is no absolute 'tell' [verbal or nonverbal signal] to lying. Having said that, there are signals that would determine that an individual is experiencing a heightened level of either anxiety or arousal, which, when compared to his or her baseline behavior, would indicate deception."

Lying creates stress, and, in the long run, stress can lead to many serious ailments, including cancer, heart disease, and diabetes. Sure, lying about a traffic jam that made you late to work isn't going to give you a tumor, but the big whoppers will weigh on your soul, your health, and your life. As my mom has always said, "You grow into your face, who you really are. And if you're a liar, it will eventually show up on your face. Lying is like cancer, it will eat you from the inside."

It's simply hard to feel good when you're doing so much bad.

Your health is not the only thing that will improve when you get your worrisome wrongdoings off your chest. It could save your career.

In 2006, San Francisco mayor Gavin Newsom admitted to having an affair with the wife of his reelection campaign manager. He apologized to a crowd of reporters gathered in his office. "I want to make it clear that everything you've heard and read is true, and I am deeply sorry about that," he said. "I am deeply sorry, and I am accountable for what has occurred." The reason his affair came to light was that the campaign manager's wife confessed to her husband of her affair with Newsom as part of her treatment in a substance abuse program.

The mayor went on to say, "I have hurt someone I care deeply about, Alex Tourk, and his friends and family, and that is something that I have to live with and something that I am deeply sorry for." Newsom told those gathered that he had met with, and apologized to, his staff, and said he was getting treatment for alcohol abuse. He went on to say, "I am also sorry that I have let the people of San Francisco down. They expect a lot of their mayor, and, my personal lapse of judgment aside, I am committed to restoring their trust and confidence and will work very hard in the upcoming months to make sure that the business of running this city is framed appropriately."

Although people may have been disappointed by his actions, his honesty may have earned their respect. He was reelected and subsequently found love, marrying Jennifer Siebel, a thirty-four-year-old actress he met on a blind date. He resigned his position as mayor to become lieutenant governor of California in January 2011.

"Because we are human beings, we should not expect to live mistake-free lives," communications professor Mark L. Knapp told me. "But we can learn from our mistakes and . . . at times be better versions of ourselves." Most of us are forgiving people, and when someone wholeheartedly asks for our forgiveness, we find it in our hearts to give it to them.

The willingness to own up to your mistakes and accept the consequences oftentimes becomes the genesis of a rebirth. When you fess up, you are immediately on your way to being perceived as a person of integrity and ethics. People who are able to admit their shortcomings are often seen as genuine and authentic, despite their imperfections. As they say in New York, it gives you street cred.

Furthermore, when you attempt to cover up your mistake or pass the blame to someone, instead of admitting your wrongdoing, you are digging a much deeper hole. Martha Stewart, for example, didn't do the crime but was sent to prison because she tried to cover up unethical activities by lying to a federal official. Her failure to fess up and subsequent efforts to cover it up got her a one-way ticket to a federal prison.

In the digital age, where we all leave an electronic footprint, anyone can be the nosy neighbor, looking over your hedges. Believe me, what they find, they will easily share. If you have something to fess up about, do it on your own terms before someone else does it for you.

Think of President Bill Clinton. I don't believe there even would have been impeachment proceedings had he taken out the word *not* when he angrily said, "I did not have sex with that woman." It would have been horribly embarrassing for him, but, ironically, by confessing he would have taken the moral high ground and made it politically much harder for his opponents to bring the impeachment charges.

I recently had to chuckle when actor George Clooney was asked by *Newsweek* magazine whether he would ever enter politics. He said that he hadn't lived his life in such a way that would make him a suitable political candidate, having been with too many women and done too many drugs. "That's the truth," he said, adding that he believed a smart campaigner "would start from the beginning by saying, 'I did it all. I drank the bong water. Now, let's talk about issues.' That's gonna be my campaign slogan: 'I drank the bong water.'"

In a 2010 Pew survey, 80 percent of Americans said that they don't trust Washington. "Trust in government rarely gets this low," said Andrew Kohut, the director of the nonpartisan Pew research center. "Politics has poisoned the well." What has happened to the well? Dishonesty in Washington.

Some people believe that if politicians told the truth, they could never get elected. I believe it would be a refreshing change. Americans aren't currently impressed with the jobs that many of their politicians are doing. In fact, in the thirty years that the Gallup Organization has tracked America's assessment of congressional job performance, 2010 revealed our lowest approval rating in history. An 83 percent disapproval rating can't be explained by our pessimism alone.

With his great humanitarian efforts and with his personal confession out of the way, George Clooney would have my vote. Everyone makes mistakes. It's how we deal with those mistakes that defines who we are.

In the late 1950s, quiz shows filled the primetime schedule. One of the most popular programs was *Twenty-one*, in which two contestants, a champion and an opponent, were placed in separate isolation booths wearing headphones, so they could neither see nor hear each other or the audience. The objective of the game was to answer a series of questions of varying difficulty, valued from 1 to 11 points, with the most difficult questions having the higher point value. The winner was the first to score a total of 21 points.

As in television today, every network wanted its shows to be watched by the most people in order to gain the highest ratings. *Twenty-one*'s ratings were lagging because the show had a reigning champion whom no one could beat. Enter Charles Van Doren, an instructor at Columbia University's English department and the son of a Pulitzer Prize winning poet, who was chosen as a contestant and who had a fourteen-week run on the show. It became a ratings bonanza. Little did the viewing audience know that the producers had coached Van Doren with the correct answers and on how to act and speak appropriately to seem believable. He became a huge celebrity, receiving thousands of letters from fans and dozens of requests to make speeches and appear in movies.

After he had appeared on the show several times, Van Doren began to feel guilty and asked the producers to let him leave the show. They eventually agreed but said it would take some time to be arranged, because Van Doren would need to be defeated in a dramatic manner. Soon after his arranged loss, Van Doren denied any improper activities when the former champion charged that some quiz shows, including *Twenty-one*, were rigged. In January 1959, Charles Van Doren was called to testify before a grand jury and still denied any involvement in fixing the outcome of the show.

Within months, it had become a full-blown national scandal. By the time Van Doren was called to testify before a congressional subcommittee, the guilt had overtaken him. His life was crumbling around him. "I knew now that I could not lie anymore, nor did I want to," Van Doren testified. "There was one way out, which I had, of course, often considered, and that was simply to tell the truth. But as long as I was trying to protect only myself and my reputation and, as I thought, the faith people had in me, I could not believe that was possible. But I was coming closer and closer to a true understanding of my position. I was beginning to realize what I should have known before, that the truth is always the best way, indeed it is the only way, to promote and protect faith. And the truth is the only thing with which a man can live. My father had told me this, even though he did not know the truth in my case. I think he didn't care what it was, so long as I told it. Other people said the same thing, even though they, too, did not know what the truth was. In the end, it was a small thing that tipped the scales. A letter came to me, which I read. It was from a woman, a complete stranger, who had seen me on the Garroway show, and who said she admired my work there. She told me that the only way I could ever live with myself and make up for what I had done—of course, she, too, did not know exactly what that was—was to admit it, clearly, openly, truly."

As a result of his honest testimony, Van Doren received a suspended sentence for lying to the grand jury. The lifted burden gave him the sudden freedom to serve as editor of the *Encyclopedia Britannica* for twenty years, as well as to write books on world history and the evolution of knowledge.

I've seen the same thing happen in the legal system. If you fess up, it will help you. If you don't, you'll be punished more severely. When I was a prosecutor, before taking something to trial, I would have what I called the "Come to Jesus" meeting with the defendant. I would ask defendants to be honest with me and to tell me what they did before I took it to trial, promising them that if they told the truth, I would cut them a much better deal. In the legal system, this is what's known as a plea bargain.

Not every crime can be taken to trial; doing so would bank-rupt the economy. The reward system for coming clean and saying, "I did it," is a reduced punishment. I frequently found that blue-collar criminals often admitted their crimes, while many of the white-collar guys thought that they could fool the jury. Generally, they couldn't. Because of their lies and inability to admit wrongdoing, they faced an angry judge and an angry jury, who tended to show no mercy when criminals continued to be obstinate about their mistakes.

I remember the case of a travel broker in Washington state who sold Catholic priests and their parishioners tour packages to the holy land. He took one or two of these trips with the priests and used their testimonials to get other, bigger groups to sign up for the trips. Everyone believed him and held church fundraisers and bake sales to help fund his trips. Children even donated their allowance savings so that their parents could take the trips! It was a classic Ponzi scheme.

When the time came to travel, he gave them excuse after excuse: "We can't get the flight we wanted," or "The hotel was booked." He'd say, "I'm fixing the problem." He expanded his travel tours and the scheme to World War II veterans, promis-ing them trips to Germany and Japan. Again, he would take only one or two trips and then book more and more groups for trips they weren't going to take.

By the time the guy got to me, he had bilked millions of dol-lars from these religious and elderly people. I couldn't bring back their money, because he'd spent it all, but I could try to give them back some dignity. Because the victims were old and because traveling to Seattle, where the trial would take place, would have been a hardship for them, I offered the defendant a plea deal—three years of jail time if he pled guilty before trial and apolo-gized to the people he had cheated. He said no. He said no all the way to the courthouse steps on the day of trial. Then he said yes. Well, too little, too late. I had already prepared for the trial, and the government had flown out his victims from all over the country and placed them in hotels for several days. I said no. A twenty-year sentence later, I'll bet he regrets not fessing up.

In other cases, such as domestic violence cases, where there is so much emotion involved, and bank robberies with the defendants caught on surveillance tape, the parties were often willing to plead guilty. I once had a big human trafficking case in which twelve defendants had smuggled thousands of illegal immigrants over the years and gotten them green cards from undercover immigration agents. I presented them with a deal. "If you come clean, I'll recommend the medium sentence, rather than the maximum," I told them. "If you don't, we'll see what a jury thinks about your crimes." All twelve of them fessed up and got hefty sentences but not what they would have, had they continued to deny their crimes.

"If you feel guilty," Dr. Dale Archer explained, "most people will analyze the situation consciously and subconsciously. What is the burden to them? The majority of people hate living with the lie, and a lot of times they decide they have to come clean. I'd rather take the consequences than live with the lie."

While I was in law school, my friend Belinda confided in me about the trouble she was having with her husband, also a graduate student. The romance had gone out of their relationship. She said he was too focused on his work and not on their relationship. She had started thinking about cheating on him and confessed to me that she had in fact kissed another man at the job she had that summer. She felt a tremendous amount of guilt for it but also a sense of despair that maybe her marriage was over. She hadn't told her husband any of this. I listened to her, asked her whether she still loved her husband, and listened to her again. Soon afterward, Belinda reconciled with her husband. But here's the surprise (at least, to me): she avoided me after that. She wouldn't look me in the eye. She turned the other way if she saw me in the hall. Only years later did I realize that she was avoiding me because she was embarrassed of the truth she had told me and had not told her husband. Seeing me brought back the guilt of her painful truth. Not telling her husband was weighing her down.

When you've done wrong and are faced with someone who has the facts against you, it is crazy thinking not to admit your mistakes. Whether it's your wife, your boss, or the law, not doing so is self-centered and egocentric. The trick is to acknowledge your mistakes, face the fear, and deal with the consequences. It is always better to work toward correcting your errors, not continuing them.

In an interview with *Esquire* magazine, Yoko Ono said that revealing the truth is always positive. "Once the truth comes out," she said, "it's all right. We're scared that if the truth comes out, that it's not all right. It's the other way around." From my experience, both in the courtroom and in my personal life, I couldn't agree more.

Yes, "sorry" is hard to say, but expressing it is often the one thing that will save you, whether in love, politics, business, or life. A friend once joked, "There's nothing worse than the moment in an argument when you realize you're wrong." So true! There's nothing that you want to do more when you know you're wrong than to run and hide.

Yes, as Elton John sings, "Sorry seems to be the hardest word," but there's also nothing better than when you admit your mistake, are forgiven for it, and are finally freed from it.

A relationship can survive even the most severe mistakes and negative actions—such as infidelity—if there is a sincere apology and sincere forgiveness. "A relationship can survive when trust is lost," "Dating Detective" Dan Crum told me. "Obviously, trust is key in any successful relationship, but since it must be earned, it can be re-earned when it is lost. "

Yet as the old cowboy saying goes, "If you find yourself in a hole, the first thing to do is stop digging."

And if you're using The Truth Advantage, someone might even give you a hand up.

So, how do you muster the courage to have the "I messed up" conversation?

**Apologize and mean it.** Nothing is better than when someone tells you, "You're right." Everyone can deal with mistakes, if you recognize them, claim them, and express genuine contrition. Starting with the words "I'm sorry" is the opening salvo toward a successful outcome.

Approximately thirty states now have some form of "apology law." These laws prevent an apology from being used against a defendant as evidence in court. Why? Because apologies are important in making something better and don't always have to indicate blame or fault. In court, an apology law allows the accused wrongdoer to express sorrow or regret about a situation and does not allow the other side to say, "If you're sorry, you're to blame."

If you've done something wrong that is personal, don't make your apology impersonal. If you can, meet the party you have offended face-to-face. It shows effort and a true willingness to put yourself on the line. Apologizing via e-mail is cold and detached, not to mention a cop-out. Unless you're face-to-face with someone, you can't really tell whether your apology was accepted.

If your mistake was unintentional, say so. But don't say you're sorry just because you think that's what the other person wants to hear. No one wants a faux apology. No one wants you to play martyr. People can tell if you're emoting or acting phony. Sincerity is the first step toward rebuilding lost trust. What the other person wants is for you to take responsibility for your actions. It's not "I'm sorry you were offended," it's "I'm sorry for offending you."

**Explain.** Unless you were simply careless in your actions, you should have a definite idea of why you did what you did.

Tell the person exactly what happened. Don't be shy. Lay it on the line. Explaining isn't about making excuses, it's about giving someone a context to understand your actions.

Let's say you missed a deadline at work. The truth is that you were up all night taking care of your sick child, who couldn't stop throwing up. Or, perhaps you were late to work because your car wouldn't start or the trains were running late. These are valid, reasonable explanations that your boss can understand. But be careful: using the same explanation over and over turns it into a careless cop-out.

**Correct.** Be prepared to say exactly how you are going to make the situation right, make restitution, and correct the mistake. If your contractor painted your room the wrong color, all you need to hear is that he'll fix it right away by painting it the right color and by not charging you for the second paint job. If you made someone a promise that you failed to keep, put yourself in his or her shoes, and ask yourself how you would feel. If the situation were reversed, what could the person do to right the wrong? That will give you an idea of the course of action you should take. Once you've explained how your error will be corrected, it's also important to ask, "Is there anything else I can do to make it right?"

**Reassure.** It will move someone more quickly to forgive you if you not only take ownership of your mistake and correct it, but if you also let him or her know how you are going to avoid making a similar mistake in the future. Assure the person that you will not make the same mistake twice, and understand that if you do make the mistake again, he or she won't be as inclined to forgive you. Remember the adage "Fool me once, shame on you; fool me twice, shame on me."

**Accept the consequences**. If you lose your job, your client, or a friendship, take your lumps. Lick your wounds and move forward. Yes, it's hard, but, as they say, what doesn't kill you makes you stronger. Next time, you'll be less likely to head down that road again. You'll still be able to keep your head held high, knowing that you did everything you could to rectify the damage done.

In the end, fessing up will give you self-confidence, clarity of values, and knowledge of who you really are. Furthermore, there will not be a ghost in the closet waiting to come out and scare you.

Now it's time to live the truth.

---

## THE TRUTH ADVANTAGE CHECKUP
### *My Bad!*

**Don't make two mistakes in a row.**
- Realize that someone is likely to forgive you for messing up once. You're only human.
- Know that by confessing your shortcomings, your truth will be more easily accepted.
- Realize that if you don't 'fess up, you are making a second mistake.

**You won't forget it.**
- Realize that even when you try to push your guilt to the back of your mind, your body will know—and suffer.
- Know that stress caused by lying and keeping secrets has been proved to lead to significant negative health implications in the future.
- Note that if your mind is full of worry, you're not making progress in your life.

**It's never too late.**
- Realize that even though you shouldn't have waited years to reveal an ill-harbored lie, later is still better than never!
- Know that if you find the courage to finally confess something, you will gain the respect of the people around you.
- Note that even though "sorry" may be the hardest word, "I forgive you" may be the three sweetest ones.

---

# CHAPTER 12

# Key 7: Live the Truth

*Fear not the path of truth for the lack of people
walking on it.*

—ARABIC PROVERB

A friend of mine was out on a blind date. She had been set up by a mutual friend, and the date seemed to be going well . . . until the guy told her, "On a scale of 1–10, I'd say you're a 6. I've been with some really attractive women." Needless to say, my friend was absolutely horrified. "What's wrong with me?" she wondered. Furthermore, what would compel a person to say something so rude? Talk about brutal honesty.

In his book *Radical Honesty*, psychotherapist Brad Blanton coaches that we should all escape the jail of our minds and say exactly what we feel to friends, spouses, and bosses. His theory is a take-no-prisoners approach to honesty.

University of Texas professor of communication Dr. Mark L. Knapp, the author of the book *An Introduction to Interpersonal*

*Communication*, told me, "The so-called radical honesty movement claims to tell the whole truth no matter what the situation. I not only don't think they do that, I don't think they are successful communicators. Catharsis may be more important to them than persuading others or even maintaining friendships."

When I read the book *Radical Honesty*, I kept thinking of the Jack Nicholson character in *A Few Good Men*: "The truth. You can't handle the truth!" Radical honesty does espouse being truthful, but if we indeed indiscriminately mouthed every thought—however hurtful—we'd be considered egomaniacal, self-centered jerks. We certainly would not be winning any friends. If you're not Simon Cowell, I would suggest practicing the principles of radical honesty with caution. You might have something thrown at you!

I think honesty can be kinder, more gentle, and much more effective. Or as Khalil Gibran, the author of *The Prophet*, said, "If indeed you must be candid, be candid beautifully."

So, back to my friend who was sitting at the table across from the blind date who had just told her that she was a 6 on the pretty scale, and that he, Mr. Suave and Debonair, had dated women far more attractive. Though he probably felt that he was "just being honest" with her, he certainly wasn't going to get anywhere with that line. He was not coming from a good place, and certainly didn't have The Truth Advantage on his side for a second date.

Having dated a passive-aggressive man before, my friend instantly smelled trouble. "He had no clue that what he said to me was inappropriate," she said. "It's classic passive-aggressive. He was using me to indirectly express his anger about something else in his life. Maybe he had a bad mother, and he's out to get back at women. I decided not to even address it with him. I didn't want to be hurt further, and I was sure he'd never acknowledge that his statement was born from some

unconsciously buried anger. Whatever the case, it was a billboard that screamed, 'You're sitting across from a jerk!'"

Even if that was his truthful opinion—that my friend wasn't
as attractive as other women he'd dated—what did he think the
statement was going to get him? Did he think it was somehow
going to help her suddenly transform herself into a supermodel? No. He was simply cutting her down. Perhaps he had
already decided that he wasn't interested in furthering the relationship, but, even still, did he need to be cruel? What good
would his statement do for either of them? Maybe he thought
he was just being funny or teasing her affectionately? Such a
harsh judgment isn't funny. It hurts. Regardless of his intent,
what he had said was, "You're not worthy." He had crushed her
feelings and made her feel bad about herself, the exact opposite
of what the truth should be used to do.

Instead, if he had to comment on her appearance, he could
have said something constructive, such as, "I think you'd look
really good with your hair up." He'd be genuinely expressing a
preference, without being offensive. Making the global statement about her overall attractiveness, as compared to other
women he'd dated, gave her nothing constructive that she
could take home. She had nowhere to go but out the door.

Let me give you another example. A friend recently
recounted a story in which a brunch with girlfriends had gone
awry when one of the women said to another, "I think you
could use some lipo." Why would she announce such a harsh
thought? If she was indeed concerned about her friend's weight,
she should have also been concerned about her friend's feelings. Rather than making a rude, unconstructive statement in
the presence of other people, she could have pulled her friend
aside at another time and discussed it in private. Then she could
have said something a little kinder and more helpful, such as
talking about the diet that she was on and asking her friend
whether she'd be interested in doing it as well. Or, she could

have invited her friend to join her on her morning run. Either of those suggestions would have invited a conversation. Instead, she had done everything a good friend wouldn't do with the truth. She had used the truth as a weapon, not as a tool.

This kind of brutal honesty is not only limited to personal life. I've seen it on a professional level, too. Once, I witnessed a television producer tell an intern, "The only thing you'll be good for in the television news business will be taking out the garbage." The intent of the producer wasn't to get the job done or help the intern learn; it was to crush the spirit of a young journalist. The look on the intern's face told me everything I needed to know. An emergency intervention was necessary, stat. I decided to quickly find something to bolster the intern's confidence before he gave up his dream. I pulled him aside and said, "I think you have a lot of potential. How about helping me with this column I'm working on?" I wasn't surprised when the young man dedicated a great deal of passion to helping me, and in the end, we turned out an excellent column. He, like the rest of us, just needed respect, and, the truth is, respect isn't hard to give.

Alicia, a twenty-five-year-old in New York, wrote in the comments on her Truth Survey: "My boyfriend thinks he's being funny by telling me that I'm a dumb blonde anytime I don't know something or make a mistake. He's not going to think it's funny when I say the dumb blonde is out the door."

"You're dumb." "You're fat." "You're ugly." "You're going bald." "Your breath stinks." No matter how true we think any of these statements are, none of these thoughts are going to get us anything but an enemy.

This type of "radical honesty" is not the truth I am suggesting you try more of. It's unkind and unnecessary, and rather than helping foster genuine communication, it hinders it. I'm also not suggesting that we walk through life tiptoeing on eggshells, worried and overthinking everything we say. The Truth Advantage is about speaking your truth with confidence, but also in an appropriate and respectful manner that moves relationships forward and strengthens, rather than weakens, them.

In college I had a dear friend, Elizabeth, who is kind, beautiful, smart, funny, loyal . . . and she has epilepsy. Even though she takes medication to keep it under control, it did and will, throughout her life, hit her at the most unexpected times. If you've ever seen someone going through an epileptic seizure, you know how scary that is. The person having the seizure has absolutely no control and is in danger of dying during each seizure.

After college, Elizabeth and I drifted apart a bit. Elizabeth went into finance and was making a big career for herself. Yet we talked on the phone and stayed in touch. She eventually told me about the man of her dreams, and I couldn't wait to meet him. A few months later, Elizabeth and Man of Dreams, "MOD," came to visit me for a weekend. We went out for a Chinese dinner, saw a movie, took a hike, and hung out and watched TV. MOD was extremely good-looking and very charming to me, his host, but not with Elizabeth.

He criticized the color and cut of her hair, how she was too slow on our hike, how she wore too much makeup, how she should really "lay off the pie." Elizabeth just smiled, as if it didn't bother her. Midway through the weekend, she pulled me aside, asking, Wasn't MOD just fabulous? I cringed, but I didn't say anything. I didn't want to lose my friend.

On Sunday, we went window shopping. I was a poor law school student, so I mean really window shopping, as in: "I couldn't afford to buy anything." But MOD went real shopping on Elizabeth's credit card—the same one he'd used to pay for their movie tickets and their dinner. He didn't even think about buying Elizabeth so much as a CD. And then he criticized her in front of me for not being ambitious enough, for not making enough money. Meanwhile, MOD didn't have a job.

Sunday night came. I asked Elizabeth to go for a walk with me, alone. And I said, "Elizabeth, you are my dear friend. And I realize I may lose you as my friend, but I have to tell you that MOD is bad for you. He criticizes everything you do. He demeans you in front of your friend, and he's taking financial advantage of you. I know that having epilepsy is frightening, but I don't want your condition or anything else to let you settle for someone who really isn't the man of your dreams! I know I risk losing you as my friend for being so honest, but I feel that as your true friend I owe that to you."

Elizabeth broke up with MOD the next day and a few years later met and married a kind and emotionally supportive man. Happily, Elizabeth and I are still friends.

However honest it may be, living the truth isn't about being mean—throwing an insult or saying something cruel. Instead, the idea is to learn how to present the truth in as kind and constructive a manner as possible. As Mahatma Gandhi said, "A man of truth must always be a man of care."

How do we become people who care? How do we live the truth kindly?

Here's the big truth secret: the only way to attain what we want in life is with the support and respect of others, and no one likes or respects a mean or dishonest person. If we want to be well liked, respected, and successful, we must be both genuine and considerate. I don't know about you, but I don't want to go to my grave with people thinking, "Good riddance." You, too, are probably hoping that your eulogy will be complimentary, that people will have something nice to say.

What type of person are you attracted to? I know I want people around me who are sincere and who tell me the truth, but who do so in a way that helps me, not hurts me. I also know that life is a two-way street, and I want to be that person for others.

It's easy to criticize, complain, or judge, but there's a bigger payoff in helping, understanding, and encouraging.

So, where do we stand with the truth?

We've . . .

- **Looked in the mirror:** We've asked ourselves, "Who am I?" and "Who do I want to be?"

- **Listened up:** We've been open and heard what others are saying.

- **Got our facts straight:** We've gathered information to base our thinking on.

- **Timed it right:** We've found the right time and place to speak up.

- **Thought our words through:** We're ready to present our truth from the right place and for the right reason.

- **Admitted our mistakes:** We've 'fessed up, owned up to what we've done and where we're coming from.

Now it's time to communicate the truth and create dynamic relationships, whether at home, at work, or at play.

Instead of thinking that you're going to "tell it like it is," think, "I want to come to the truth." By being honest and working toward positive results, you will help others see, grow, and excel, and in return, others will help you do the same.

The truth, if well delivered, will give you greater peace of mind, greater success, and ultimate happiness.


# Worst First

Let's start with the worst, the hardest truth you would ever have to deliver. If you can deliver the worst truth, everything shy of that will seem easily attainable.

If your loved one is serving in the armed forces, getting a knock on the door and seeing a military official on your steps is perhaps your greatest fear. Telling a soldier's next of kin that their brave serviceman or -woman has been killed in the line of duty is something that, sadly, people in the military have to do every day. Military chaplain Norris Burkes wrote about the experience of delivering hard truths for the Christian Broadcasting Network. He says that no matter how many times he's had to deliver the news, he always sticks with the "We regret to inform you" script. His goal? To be compassionate yet professional and to "get through without cracking." Then, after telling that sad truth, he feels his job is to provide the needed comfort.

Chaplain Burkes says the death notification team, composed of a lawyer, a chaplain, a medic, and a commander, rehearses the script and even watches a video that explains the process. The training video details one such tragic scene. A little boy playing in his driveway sees a blue sedan pull up. His mother comes out of the garage, wiping oil from her hands. She asks, "Can I help you?" but, on seeing the uniforms, realizes the harsh reality. The commander asks whether they can go inside. "Come back later," she says. "This isn't a good time." The commander explains that they have to speak now.

Inside the house, the commander begins his script. "Are you Mrs. Fred T. Smith?" "Yes." "Is your husband Captain Fred T. Smith?" "Yes." "Ma'am, we regret to inform you that your husband Captain Fred T. Smith, Social Security number 555–55–5555, was killed."

Chaplain Burkes says that they never make it through the script "without a gush of sobbing and a hemorrhage of denial." Each member of the death notification team then performs his specific duty: the medic watches for possible signs of fainting, the lawyer explains how a trusted friend will accompany the soldier on his way home, and the chaplain holds the loved one's hand and prays. There is only one guiding principle through-out the entire process: compassion.

# Bad News

There are other words that we all hope we will never hear. "You have three months to live." "I'm leaving you." "You're fired." No conversation can shake you to the core as much as one that begins with, "I'm so sorry to have to tell you this, but . . ." Whether you are being informed of a terminal illness, the end of your marriage, or the loss of your job, these are the toughest truths to both say and hear.

Yet with a little compassion on the truth teller's part, all of these things can be easier to swallow. Any truth to be received well must be told with consideration.

How does a doctor find the right words to break bad medi-cal news?

I know an obstetrician who specializes in high-risk preg-nancies. In the course of a single day, he delivers the most joy-ous news, as well as the most tragic. In one examination room, he gets to tell a mother that she's expecting healthy twins; in another, he has to inform a mother of the horrible news that she has lost her baby. The wails that come from his examination rooms can often be heard down the halls of the hospital. When I asked him how he delivers such painful news, he said, "I just try to be empathetic. In the beginning, I would imagine that the mother I was speaking with was my own sister, and I'd tell her the news the same way I'd want someone to tell my sister. It's all about compassion."

He pointed me to the work of Dr. Robert Buckman, an oncol-ogist at the University of Toronto. Dr. Buckman developed a sys-tem of delivering bad news, which he believes to work not only in the health-care setting but also for other bad-news scenarios, from firing someone to explaining divorce to a child. Dr. Buckman's book *How to Break Bad News* introduced a six-step protocol that he later refined to what he now calls the S-P-I-K-E-S strategy.

**(S) Setting**: Never deliver bad news over the telephone. Bad news should be delivered face-to-face in as private an area as possible, free of distractions. Dr. Buckman suggests starting the conversation with a simple question, such as "How are you feeling today?" Then, he says, just sit back and listen. Let the person know you care about his or her feelings.

**(P) Perception**: See how much the person already knows or suspects. By figuring out what his or her mind-set is, you'll know where to start your explanation.

**(I) Invitation**: People want varying degrees of the truth. Some people want to know every detail, and others want only the gist. Determine how much the person you're talking to wants to know.

**(K) Knowledge**: Prepare the person for the news by starting with, "I'm sorry to have to tell you this," or, "I wish I had better news to tell you." From there, take it one step at a time. Don't throw every detail at the person immediately. Instead, roll it out gradually: give a bit of information, assess the person's response, and give a little more. Make sure you go at his or her pace, not at yours. If the person starts to cry, take a minute to help him or her through it before moving on. Above all, Dr. Buckman says that you should remain calm, even when the other person isn't.

**(E) Empathy**: Unless you have actually been through a similar situation, don't attempt to comfort the person by saying, "I know how you feel." It's offensive. Instead, acknowledge that the news is very distressing and that the person can look to you for support. Dr. Buckman suggests saying something like, "I have never had to walk in your shoes and hope that I never will, but I can help you through this."

**(S) Strategy and summarize**: Review what you have just told the person, and clarify any information he or she is unsure about. When you are certain the person has fully grasped the news, chart your course forward for how you're going to tackle the situation. Also, make it clear that you will be there for the person, and invite him or her to talk to you whenever the need arises.

Hopefully, you'll never be in the position of having to tell someone or hear about such a harsh reality. Yet during the course of our lives, all of us will have to hear or deliver bad news of some kind. Whether you're getting fired or doing the firing, being on either side of the desk is a tough spot. It's not as easy as Donald Trump makes it seem on his television show *The Apprentice.* If you have The Truth Advantage on your side, however, the burden will be significantly lessened.

Ask any manager or boss, and most employers will probably tell you that firing is their least favorite part of the job. It is an unfriendly, uncomfortable, and disagreeable moment for both parties involved. Unfortunately, it's the sad reality of business life. Sometimes, people just don't work out. Real estate guru and star of ABC's entrepreneurial show *Shark Tank*, Barbara Corcoran, tells me that when she owned her company, The Corcoran Group, her least favorite, most awkward charge was letting someone go. Yet she developed a successful technique that helped her get through the harsh task, while leaving the person being fired with his or her dignity.

The key to her technique is never giving someone bad news without some good news attached. Always start by telling the individual what he or she does well. "When you fire people," Barbara says, "you want to ensure that they leave with their self-esteem intact. You're not trying to ruin their lives. I always take the time to prepare a list of what they do well and tell them. It's easier for them to accept your critique of why they're not suited for their current job, and they'll know what their talents are when they are looking for a new job." Barbara also believes that you should just cut to the chase—no one who is getting fired wants to sit around for an hour talking about it. "But tell them the truth," she says. "Nothing is worse than being hanged when you don't know what the crime is. It's simply not fair, and it leaves the person wondering for the rest of his life."

Displaying the right body language is especially important in situations where you must tell people something they might not want to hear, and it can go a long way toward easing difficult situations. My friend Michelle, who works in human resources for a major pharmaceutical company, once related to me the importance of positive body language in her own managerial style. She agrees with Barbara that firing employees is one of the toughest tasks of running any business, but she says it's a necessary deed if you want to run a successful business.

Breaking difficult news is always a hard thing to do, but honesty, directness, and the right body language can make it much easier.

Michelle told me that whenever she has to tell employees they're being let go, she tries to be as direct as possible. That means being honest, but for her she says it means not hiding behind her desk to break the bad news. She says she always makes a point of coming around her desk and sitting next to the recipient of the bad news. Why? Because simple gestures like this make it clear that even though the news is bad, it's being delivered from a place of compassion and honesty.

By learning from these people who have delivered life's worst news, we can apply the same principles to telling the truth in our everyday lives.

## Touchy Situations

Have you ever had to deliver an awkward truth? What's the best way to tell your friend she has bad breath or something stuck in her teeth? How do you tell a colleague that he has body odor or a subordinate that what she's wearing is a little too ris-qué for the workplace?

"I think the hardest thing I've ever had to do is tell my friend she has bad breath," Wini, a seventy-one-year-old from Kansas, admitted on her Truth Survey. "I thought about it for weeks. I dreaded it, lost sleep over it. I finally decided to get her some fancy breath spray and wrapped it like a beautiful present. When I gave it to her, she said, 'Are you trying to tell me something?' And I said, 'Yes.' We both looked at each other and burst out laughing."

There are some truths in our everyday lives that aren't earth shattering but that are still difficult to say and tough to hear. Certain things, such as a coworker's bad breath, aren't nearly as hard to handle as the serious troubles in life, for example, illness or divorce, but they are still uncomfortable and have to be addressed.

In the case of a friend's stinky breath, human relations experts suggest offering your friend a mint, which is a polite but subtle way of letting your friend know her breath is less than fresh. If a person has something stuck in his teeth, discreetly pull him aside and be quick and direct. Let him know specifically where it is. Say something like, "You've got a little something stuck on your front left tooth." It'll save your friend later horror when he realizes everyone has already noticed the spinach dangling from his teeth. It's direct and honest and doesn't make a big deal of it. Most important, it gets the job done.

The same remedy applies to letting your friend know about "something" sticking out of his or her nose. Pass along a tissue and make a little hand gesture, such as tapping your nose, and hopefully the person will get the hint. If not, be direct, to the point, and get it over with. Remember, situations like this are similar to Band-Aid removal: the quicker you do it, the faster the pain is gone. As for someone with bad body odor, experts suggest asking the person whether he or she has recently changed brands of deodorant. If the person says no, try saying something like, "I really love the one I'm using, you should check it out." If your friend still doesn't get the hint, buy him or her the deodorant and deal with it honestly. Be quick and direct. You might say, "I feel that as your friend, I should tell you that I've been noticing that you've been a little less than fresh." Or simply, "I really think you should try this." Again, as in all delicate situations, tact is key and compassion is essential.

Or as psychologist and relationship expert Margaret Paul explained it, "Look at every action in terms of intent: are we speaking our truth to take loving care of other people or to control them? Understanding intent is vital to understanding the whole issue of telling your truth."

Although you may think there is sometimes no tactful way to tell people an uncomfortable truth, if you genuinely care for them, you will overcome your own discomfort to prevent even more embarrassment for them. Although it's momentarily uncomfortable, they will be glad that you cared enough to let them know and that you trust them enough to communicate with them directly. Your honesty in these situations is a gift, and by using The Truth Advantage, you're gaining a friend.

You will find in all of these circumstances that your honesty will lead to a better relationship. Why? Because telling the truth with compassion builds a good rapport.

President Lyndon B. Johnson said, "If two men agree on everything, you may be sure that one of them is doing the thinking." No two people are ever going to agree on everything—just watch me debate on the Fox News Channel sometime—and there are times that your opinion and your personal truth are going to counter the opinion, the truth, or the ideas of someone else. What do you do then?

Certainly, you can, as they say in politics and religion, "agree to disagree," but you can also use The Truth Advantage to respectfully disagree and move the relationship forward.

The big no-no's about disagreeing are

- **Being rude.** Disrespect and bad manners get you nowhere, especially if you're on opposite sides of the fence.

- **Taking the "I am right, you are wrong" stance.** If you begin any conversation by saying, "You're wrong," your unspoken statement is "Put up your dukes." It's the opening salvo for "Bring it on. Let's fight."

- **Using "ad hominem" attacks.** Personal attacks and digs—you're a cheater, a liar, fat—get you nowhere. Trying to link one characteristic to another nonrelevant issue only stirs up a hornets' nest. This is often used in politics. For example, Candidate John can't be believed on his proposals to fix the economy. He got fired from his last job. Statements such as this only cause anger.

- **Insulting the other person's intelligence.** If you want to make someone angry, go ahead and say that he or she is dumb. You can bet that for the rest of the conversation, you'll be trying to dig your way out of this mess.

We all want to be right. Unfortunately, sometimes we're not. Most of our opinions aren't random but are strongly connected to our value systems and our backgrounds. Disagreeing isn't about being angry or putting someone down. It's not meant to be hostile, and it should not be combative.

So, how do we move a conversation forward, when there are people on two opposing sides of an issue? How do we allow both sides to communicate their truths? Here's what I used in the courtroom to deal with hostile witnesses, argumentative opposing counsel, and troublesome judges and win my cases:

- **Establish an area of common ground.** By finding something to agree on, you are opening yourself up to the idea that someone with opposite views can still have other things in common with you. For example, liberals and

conservatives may approach issues from opposite ideo-
logical standpoints, but both have a common ground that
they each want America and Americans to succeed.

- **Say "yes, and . . ."** When you respond to someone by saying, "Yes, but . . ." you are communicating that you are
simply dismissing what they just said. You're drawing a
line in the sand and announcing you're on the right side,
and they are on the wrong. Saying "Yes, and . . ." opens
up the conversation to further dialogue. It moves things
forward, rather than backward.

- **Ask for clarification or amplification.** Saying, "Help me
understand," or inviting the person to give you more information shows an interest in, and a respect for, what someone
else has to say. Then, if you still disagree, you'll be disagreeing based on having looked at a full picture of someone's
position. You'll also have a greater chance of persuading
someone after you've allowed him to fully express himself.

In the end, when both sides feel that they have been heard,
they are more likely to respect each other, even if they ultimately
just have to "agree to disagree."

The Truth Advantage is not about being rude and justifying
it by saying you "just want to be honest," but it also doesn't
mean sugarcoating your opinions or being fake and sweet all of
the time. Instead, you should be genuine, yet kind.

If you can't tell the truth, don't tell a lie. If a friend asks you
the proverbial "Do I look fat in this dress?" and she does, you
know that saying yes will crush her. But don't say no, either.
Instead, try saying that perhaps the dress fits a little weird or
doesn't complement her best features. Point out what looks
right about it, such as, "It makes your legs look great," or "The
color is gorgeous," and then say it's not quite right and suggest
she try a different dress.

If your spouse is driving you crazy by leaving all of the housework for you to do, be honest with him or her. But don't start the conversation by saying, "You never do anything around the house," or "I'm sick of doing all of this by myself!" Instead, try, "I've been feeling stressed," and, "Would you please help me?" Express how the act of cooperation and kindness will help both of you.

If your friend asks you to dinner, and you simply don't feel like going, don't lie and say you have other plans. Rather, say, "That night doesn't work for me. How about a night next week instead?" If your friend presses the topic, explain honestly but politely why you don't feel like going. "I've been stressed out at work, so when I have a night off, I need to decompress." An understanding friend will accept your explanation. I once told a friend who was enthusiastically helping me build a deck on my house that I needed "a little time to decompose." Not exactly what I meant to say, but he got the point—I had to take a break—and we both had a few laughs.

We parents aren't perfect, no matter how hard we try to be. I've found that "Because I said so" fails to satisfy a child's question every time, and it also makes children feel as if their feelings are being dismissed. If your child asks you to hang out with a friend whom you might consider a bad influence, be honest with him or her. Don't criticize your own children for their desire to have friends or fun. Instead, explain your concerns and make the time to discuss the exact issues that bother you, and then point out the good qualities in a friend whom you do like.

"Dr. Love" Leo Buscaglia once said, "Too often we underestimate the power of a touch, a smile, a kind word, a listening ear, an honest compliment, or the smallest act of caring, all of which have the potential to turn a life around."

When you're living the truth, don't hide behind the word *truth* to recklessly hurt people's feelings. At the end of the day, we don't want to forget to be decent human beings.

The easiest and simplest way to question whether the truth that's coming out of your mouth is one that you can live by is to rely on one of the best biblical charges: "Do unto others as you would have them do unto you." Before you say something, ask yourself whether you'd want it said to you.

"We don't need to be good all the time to be good people," explained Dr. Mark Knapp, "but we need to struggle toward that goal." We want to be better. We want to be kind. We want to be heard. We want to be respected.

If you hope to achieve those goals, when you're telling the truth you should leave other people's self-esteem intact. In being forthright, you don't have to destroy someone's self-confidence or inflict emotional harm in order to get your point across.

I received a package in the mail today that said, "Fragile. Handle with care," and I thought about ripping the label off and wearing it on my lapel. We're all fragile . . . and we each want to be handled with care. So, even though sometimes the truth does hurt, there is still always a way to deliver the message that is constructive and compassionate. And there's also a definite bad way.

In telling a difficult truth, find a style and a manner that work for you. I generally pair a problem with a solution. I remember that when Jacob was a high school freshman, he was determined to take advanced placement math, but it was a real struggle. He was staying up past 2 a.m. on many nights to study. He lost his appetite and was really getting distressed. He was in a big public school class, and the teacher just didn't have time to explain some of the math concepts that stymied him. I was no help. So, one night in October, I said, "Jacob, you're doing a lot. You're taking advanced placement French and English, as well as playing baseball and being in the school band. I think what this math class is doing to you is not good for you, and it's not good for our family. Here's an idea: I've found a tutor. Let's try her out and see what happens. If you are doing better and, more important, are happier by Thanksgiving, you can stay in the class. If not, let's agree that you'll go to regular math and be just fine." We shook on it. Three years later, my son has been accepted to MIT, and his tutor (and mom) couldn't be prouder.

If delivering a difficult truth is causing you problems, find a solution or something that will improve the situation before you deliver it.

Here's another way to think of it. Pair something bad with something good. We all have times when the honest answer is to say no to a request—such as being asked to dinner or to a party we don't want to attend. Situations like this present a problem for a lot of us because we hate to let people down. The solution is to realize that someone else will get to say yes and will appreciate the opportunity to go.

There are lots of times when we can make lemonade out of lemons. If we can't afford a winter vacation this year, I have told my kids that we "get" to stay home and relax . . . have nice fires, popcorn and movies, and just enjoy some downtime together. Of course, pairing something bad with something good is not always possible because there are times when things are just plain bad. They can't be glossed over. Acknowledge them as they are, but be thoughtful enough to add extra compassion.

This is, after all, a "self-help" book. You must take responsibility and be accountable for what you do and say. It is up to you to align your words, thoughts, and deeds so that you're kind, even when the news isn't. Stand proudly on your words. If you want to help yourself out, be honest in your dealings with others and deliver your truth from a good place in your heart.

Try this experiment: Take the opportunity to tell someone a truthful kindness today. The action and the sentiment will go a long way not only for the recipient of your kindness, but for you, too. And perhaps, if it's true that kindness begets kindness, these small kindnesses will ripple out like the little pebble tossed in a pond.

**Give your boss a raise:** Tell him why you like working with him.

**Boost your child's spirit:** Tell your son you've noticed how handsomely he's been dressing.

**Toss a truth to someone you don't know:** Tell the cashier at the grocery store that you like her earrings.

**Give a compliment to a loved one:** Tell your partner why you're thankful you found his or her love.

The positive results you achieve with each of these small tokens will inspire you. I'm betting you'll be so inspired that you'll want to try giving a few truthful kindnesses tomorrow, too. Then, you'll probably give it a go the day after that. Three days in a row will make it a happy habit. You'll receive satisfaction inside and out, and you'll discover that people will suddenly want to help you achieve your dreams.

No one wants a spouse, a coworker, or a friend who says one thing but does another. We generally know whether someone is a person of his word. You want to be that person, the one who walks the walk. If you're consistent in doing what you say and saying what you mean, you will develop authentic, meaningful relationships in all areas of your life. Honesty is the key to living a fulfilling life that inspires everyone around you.

Most of us want to do the right thing, but, yes, we sometimes succumb to temptation or do things we regret. We're human. None of us is perfect. We all have moments when we go on automatic pilot and say and do things we don't mean, something as simple as, "I'll e-mail you tomorrow." Yet by living as true to our word as possible—by showing up, following through, and being good for our word—we build trust with others. If we live by the same rules we set for others, don't make promises we can't keep, and keep the ones we do make, we become beacons of integrity, reliability, and personal strength.

I hope that you have come to see that by living the truth—by being consistent in what you say and do—you are not only more deeply respected but also more deeply loved.

If each of us treats those we encounter with respect and compassion, not only will the world we live in be a better place, but you'll personally find that you'll earn a reputation as a person of goodness and integrity. The results will be dramatic. Living the truth will make you happier, healthier, and more successful in all that you do. Furthermore, you'll be able to put your head on the pillow at night and sleep well and wake up each morning to face each new day living The Truth Advantage.

---

## THE TRUTH ADVANTAGE CHECKUP

### *Don't just think it, do it!*

**Ditch the brutal honesty.**

- Realize that no one needs to know or hear every thought that pops into your mind.
- Before you say something "painfully" truthful, ask yourself what your intentions are.
- Know that if your words are intended only to harm someone, the "truth" should be rethought.

**Some truths may be tough to tell—but you have to tell them.**

- Realize that no matter what your truth is, there is a right way to tell it.
- Make sure you've thought through what that right way is.

- Have a dress rehearsal and practice saying it aloud before you have to say it for real.

**Respect others' truths.**

- Realize that expressing the truth doesn't mean trying to trump another person.
- Know that by presenting your personal truth, you are saying to someone else, "I trust you."
- Note that when you truly listen and respect the truths of others, they truly respect you.

# PART FOUR

# Unlocking the Advantage

*Kind words will unlock an iron door.*

—TURKISH PROVERB

# CHAPTER 13

# How to Deal with Lies and Liars

*The way to overcome the angry man is with gentleness, the evil man with goodness, the miser with generosity, and the liar with truth.*

—INDIAN PROVERB

In answer to my American Truth Survey, numerous respondents noted that they were often angriest when someone close to them said he or she was going to do one thing but then did another.

"My biggest pet peeve," a fifty-one-year-old woman in Kansas wrote, "is when my husband says he's going to be home at a certain time and then arrives home an hour late without calling. How can he not see that I'd be worried, wondering, or concerned? After almost twenty years of marriage, we still have huge fights over it. I consider that a lie."

This is like a broken contract. One reason I think that the number of lawyers has increased so exponentially during the last few years is because we've become a society of people who are not willing to be true to our word. We've become numb to broken contracts, forgotten appointments, and promises not kept. Broken trust has almost become the norm.

So, how do we encourage others to make truth their advantage?

Now that you've learned how to live honestly and detect untruth in others, it's time to put that knowledge to use. The realization that a friend, a loved one, or a coworker is not being honest with you can be painful, but it can also be an opportunity. Using The Truth Advantage, you can find effective ways to approach and resolve the situation and implement helpful strategies to deal with a person who isn't being completely honest with you.

**Try to listen first.** Rather than just jumping in with your accusation, first say something like, "I felt worried about where you were so late last night. I know you said you were studying with friends, but you didn't get home until after midnight. Is everything alright?" Remember: the point isn't to catch the person in another lie. Instead, listening a bit more may give him or her another chance to come through with the truth, and it puts that person in the position of explaining what happened (rather than thrusting you into a position of outright accusation and recrimination).

Try to start by being understanding, aware that we all make mistakes. This doesn't mean you're going to condone, encourage, or allow dishonesty. It means that you're aware that we're all human, and you're going to give the person a chance to explain.

**Get to the point.** Don't beat around the bush. The person already knows something is wrong. Start with something positive about the individual, then get to the painful truth. Take the time to allow him or her to both process and respond to your statements. Allow the person to ask questions. This is how we come to terms with, and better understand, harsh realities. Address each and every one of the individual's questions back to you.

**Try to keep your sentiments framed in "I" statements.** As tempting as it might be to want to shame the other person for his or her failure to be truthful, you'll always be better off if you try instead to communicate, as clearly and objectively as possible, how his or her untruths made you feel.

Try to use "I" statements, rather than "you" statements. For instance, when your son or daughter comes home late from a drinking party and gives you the "I was at the town library going through microfiches" fib—and still doesn't admit to the lie when you give him or her the chance to do so—start by saying something like, "I am really puzzled by this. You say you were at the library, but I learned that the library isn't open on Friday nights. I feel so sad and disappointed about this situation." Avoid angrily saying things like, "You're lying to me! The library isn't even open on Friday nights. You are a disgrace to our family. You should be mortified, and, if you're not, I'll make sure you are! I'm revoking your allowance and posting your photo on the Wiehl household's Wall of Shame!"

**Compassion is key.** Be as forgiving as possible, but let the individual know that lying is unacceptable. Dr. Dale Archer says, "A relationship can survive a bald-faced lie, but trust has to be earned again. So, we are starting back at ground zero."

Let the ones who lie to you work through the emotional burden associated with their mischief. You don't need to carry this burden! You're upset with them because you believe that the truth is always a better way to go, even if it's an admission of wrongdoing.

You want the people you care about to live up to the image you have of them. You want them to be self-aware, confident, and respected by you and others. Once you've let your friend or loved one know that you realize you've been lied to, say something like, "I forgive you, but I don't find this situation acceptable. If you want my trust, I need to know that you are truthful with me—always."

Take the high road. Overdoing the guilt and shame will simply ricochet back to you through the other person's defensiveness—and then you'll feel regret for your own harshness. Again, remember, that we're all capable of lying sometimes. Treat the liar as you would want to be treated if you were caught in the same situation! By showing your grace but insisting on the truth, you'll be the one who wins the day.

**Not all lies are created equal.** Make it clear that lying is wrong. If it's your child, you may need to drive home, again, the importance of honesty. If it's an adult, you may tell the person that being upfront with you is the way to your heart, and that you'll feel much closer to him or her with a forthright and honest relationship.

Let's face it: it's one thing to have your six-year-old daughter fib about finishing her homework and quite another to learn that your husband was frolicking on a sandy beach in Maui with his female yoga instructor—when he told you he was away at a highly important business conference in Atlanta! All lies betray trust and are potentially deeply hurtful, but some are definitely more profoundly unethical or immoral than others.

So, try to save your strongest expression of disbelief and indignation for the really big lies! Even when it comes to the difficult situations of broken faith and broken hearts, try your best to follow the guidance of living truthfully.

---

TRUTH ADVANTAGE DO'S AND DON'TS!

DO Forgive people who sincerely ask for forgiveness.
DON'T say you forgive someone and not mean it.

---

None of us like to be lied to, but it happens. What I've found is that lying is like a scraped knee. You have to deal with it, clean the wound, and put a bandage on it. In time, it will heal. Yet the only way for it to get better is to address it, care for it, and move forward.

In every relationship, there are good times, great times, and some hard times. Open communication, compassion, and understanding will give you The Truth Advantage.

Now that you know the cause and effect of lies and the liars who tell them, make note of three things: (1) no good comes of lying; (2) just as you have a "lie-dar" hunch when you think others may be lying to you, they might have the same hunch when you're lying to them; and (3) just as you feel bad when others lie to you, they feel the same when you lie to them.

As the Blue Fairy said to Pinocchio, "Now, remember, Pinocchio: be a good boy. And always let your conscience be your guide."

Let's leave this lying behind and move on to have The Truth Advantage.

---

## THE TRUTH ADVANTAGE CHECKUP

### *May the Truth Be with You*

**You have control.**
- Realize that you were lied to.
- Know that you were hurt, but you don't have to be a victim.
- Note that how you choose to react to someone's dishonesty will play a large role in the outcome.

**Be kind.**
- Realize that no matter how upset you are, you want to handle it with a kind heart.
- Try to first understand the reasoning behind the person's actions.
- Note how you would have wanted him or her to deal with the situation.

**Pick your battles wisely.**

- Realize that some lies don't compare to others!
- Know the difference between lies that can be forgiven easily and those that can't.
- Note that not overreacting will make it a lot easier for both of you.

# CHAPTER 14

# The Truth Advantage in Action

*Vision without action is a daydream. Action without
vision is a nightmare.*

—JAPANESE PROVERB

A s I was finishing the manuscript for this book, my phone
rang. It was my friend Shannon, a mom who is working
hard to instill in her daughter a sense of worth, without a sense
of entitlement, and a heart that is kind, yet strong enough not to
get stomped on. Shannon was very upset.

"I need some advice," she began. "It's Leanne's softball
coach. He's done nothing but put her down. All season long,
he's only put her into play when it's the last out of the game, so
that if she strikes out, she's the fall guy. But now here it is the
last few weeks of her senior year, and he's completely ignoring
her. I've had enough. Tomorrow at the banquet when I shake
his hand, I'm going to give him the truth—that's he's a worthless

jerk and has ruined my daughter's senior year of high school."
She paused. "So, what exactly should I say?"

Hold the phone.

It was time to put The Truth Advantage into action.

"Shannon," I said, "before you give the coach a piece of your
mind, let's try something." She and I then used the "7 Keys to
Happiness and Fulfillment" to help her figure out a way to get
the truth off her chest and use it so that she'll feel positive about
the outcome.

# Key 1: Look in the Mirror

Why? Shannon needs to know exactly why this bothers her so
much. Besides the fact that she wants her daughter to enjoy
softball, what are her underlying reasons for being so angry?

"Did you play softball as a kid?" I asked her.

"No," she said. "I rode horses. I was actually a star eques-
trian. I had a big white horse that all of the judges noticed and
loved. I suppose I was on the opposite end of the spectrum from
Leanne."

It was a "KEY TRUTH ADVANTAGE moment" for Shannon.

"Wow," she said. "I've never thought about that. I want
Leanne to get to experience the same feeling of victory I felt!
She's not getting to feel what it's like to sit atop a big white
horse and have her star moment. I'm scared she's getting left on
the sidelines!"

I told her she had to forgive herself for that, and she agreed.
We moved on.

"So, what do you want to accomplish by telling the coach
that you want your daughter to have that kind of experience?"

"I would think that he would want to inspire all of his players
with that kind of moment, so that they all might have confidence

in their abilities," she said. "I mean, when you throw a girl who hasn't gotten to play all season in to hit the last out, she is going to be nervous! She steps up to bat at a major disadvantage!"

"When someone needs or feels the desire to tell you something about yourself, how do you want them to tell you?"

"Just say it!" she snapped. "Just tell me."

I reminded her she probably wouldn't want someone to call her "worthless" or a "jerk," the original names she had labeled the coach.

"You're right," she said. "I guess I'd want someone to be kind about it. I suppose I just want him to know how it feels for a young girl not to be given an opportunity. I owe that to the daughters he'll coach after mine."

She had unlocked the first door to The Truth Advantage.

# Key 2: Listen Up!

I asked Shannon whether she had talked to the coach much during the season, about this issue or anything else?

"How could I?" she asked. "He's never said one word to me!"

"Have you ever tried to say anything to him?"

"No," she admitted.

"Has Leanne?"

"At one game she did ask him if she could play, if she was going to be put in," Shannon told me.

"And?"

"He reminded her that he was the coach and she was the player."

"What did Leanne do?"

"She went back and held down the bucket," she laughed. Shannon explained that there is a large softball bucket with a lid, and Leanne often made it her perch during the games. "In fact," Shannon said, "Leanne and I joke that we know what's going to happen at the end of the season. He's going to give her the 'Sportsmanship Trophy' because she was the team's bucket-sitting cheerleader!"

Shannon said she had observed the coach's interactions with other parents all season and said she didn't want to put herself in a position of being barked at. She felt strongly that no matter what she did, the coach was just going to argue with her and tell her that he didn't need her—a player's mom—telling him how to coach. She was sure it would become a war of words that she couldn't win.

Arguing from pure emotion with someone who is in complete power won't work. Shannon decided to move on to the facts.

## Key 3: Get Your Facts Straight

The first fact Shannon needed to realize was that yelling at the coach was not going to do any good for anybody: not her, not her daughter, and certainly not the coach. He would instantly shut down, and nothing she said would be heard. He also wouldn't respond well if, rather than yelling, she quietly insulted him.

Shannon agreed.

So, I asked her to give me the unemotional truths: the stats, the numbers, the hard facts.

How often has Leanne actually gotten to play? Of a total of eight league games, Leanne had gotten to play in the last innings of three. In the scrimmage games, every time Leanne was up to bat—at least once a game—she got at least a base hit. "But when it came time for the real games," Shannon said, "he always picked the tenth grader who struck out every time."

"So, that's it?" I asked. "That's all that she's gotten to play in a whole season of softball?"

"Oh, yeah," Shannon remembered. "She's also been allowed to run a couple of times for the pitcher, who is a bad runner."

"So, only two times?"

"Maybe three," Shannon said. "But the biggest insult was that one of those times the pitcher had gotten to second, he put Leanne in, and she stole third and made it home to score the tie-breaking run."

"That should have felt like a victory, right?" I encouraged.

"Should have," she said. "We thought at least she would make the paper for helping win the game. But she didn't. The paper gave the pitcher all of the glory, saying that it was the pitcher—with her name and photo—who had stolen third and scored the winning run. They didn't even mention Leanne at all!"

"Did the coach do that?"

"I don't know that for sure," Shannon admitted. "It could have been the reporter. But I think the coach does give all of the stats, and the pitcher is the assistant coach's daughter."

That was another "KEY TRUTH ADVANTAGE moment." Perhaps another reason—nepotism?—that Leanne wasn't getting to play!

"Has Leanne done anything she knows of to rub the coach the wrong way?"

"No, not that we can figure out."

"Has Leanne always made practice on time?"

"Yes, except for the week she had a medical excuse because of her tonsils."

"Missed any games?" I grilled.

"Two games, again for her tonsils."

"And if you were to fairly access Leanne's skills against the other players, what would that be?"

"I'd say she's right in the middle," Shannon said. "Half of the team is better, half of the team is worse. But she'd be a top player if she'd gotten to play! Even the team captain has asked the coach to let Leanne go to bat."

"And?"

"He did. In the last inning."

Shannon gained the advantage using the facts.

## Key 4: Think before You Speak

Shannon was "angry mom." She admitted it, and just ask any-one who has ever experienced an angry mom—we can be like a lioness protecting her cub. "No one wants to go anywhere near a growling dog," I reminded her.

"Speaking of which," I continued, "what would you do if that local newspaper reporter happens to be at the awards ban-quet and overhears what you say? Would you want him to report about the 'angry mom who went off on the coach?'"

"Absolutely not!" she said. "But the paper probably won't be there."

"What about other moms and dads?" I asked.

"Hadn't thought about that," she admitted.

Imagining other observers witnessing your words and actions can suddenly make you quickly rethink your approach. (Next time you're thinking about treating a waiter poorly, just realize that others are watching.)

"You're right," she said. "I don't want to look like a crazy mom. All I want is for him to look at the personal impact he's had on making a girl sit game after game on the bucket and realize that every player simply deserves a chance to play."

By using the Think before You Speak key, Shannon saved herself heartache and her daughter from possible public embarrassment.

## Key 5: Time It Right

Now, let's talk about timing. "Is the awards ceremony the 'right time' to tell the coach this truth?"

"I was going to do it after the award ceremony," she explained.

"You mean, while everyone was milling about congratulating the team on the season."

"Well, I would get him when he wasn't talking to anyone and pull him aside."

"Don't you think Leanne would know what you were doing?" I asked.

"Sure," Shannon answered. "But she knows I'm going to talk to him. She wants me to say something."

"But don't you think that might make a teenage girl uncomfortable, watching her mom talk about her to her coach while she's in a room of her peers and their parents?"

Shannon decided that I was right. "But when?" she asked. "I want to get this off my chest! And how? It would make me uncomfortable to be alone in the room with him."

"Why not write him a letter?" I asked.

"That's a great idea!" she said. "Because at the end of the year, I always write letters to each of Leanne's teachers to tell them what they did for Leanne. I can tell him what he didn't do!"

"Or did do," I said. "He has shown her that she can keep a positive attitude, even in a rather lackluster situation."

It was another "KEY TRUTH ADVANTAGE moment."

Shannon got choked up. "You're right. What a good sport she is! You should see how the whole team looks to and depends on her for encouragement."

## Key 6: Admit Your Mistakes

Here's the truth: we want all our children's talents to be both nurtured and celebrated. Lady Gaga echoed in my head—"My mama told me when I was young, 'We are all born superstars . . .'"—and I flashed to my own teenage years. My mom encouraged me to join the track team because I was a very good runner. Faithfully every morning I set my alarm at five o'clock and got up to run. I remember at one very important qualifying meet the coach refused to put me into the relay team, not even in third position, which generally goes to the slowest of the four girls. I had better times than three of the four runners he had picked and pleaded my case with my coach. He told me that another girl would guarantee a win. Well, she didn't. We lost. And on the car ride home, I complained to my dad about the coach's unjust decision and bemoaned how unfair it was.

He pulled the car over and turned to look at me in the backseat. "Lis," he said, "life isn't fair." Then he turned around, put the car in drive, and drove on. I remember the moment vividly. I got home, climbed into bed, and cried my eyes out. Looking back, I realize my dad did me a big a favor. Instead of letting it slow me down, I took what I thought was the coach's unfair decision and decided to run harder. Eventually, I proved myself by setting the state's Amateur Athletic Union record in the mile run.

Not every moment is going to be fair, but it's how we handle those troublesome instances that will either propel us forward or hold us back. "Do you want Leanne to continue to play softball in college?" I asked.

"I just want Leanne to have her moment," she said, finally 'fessing up.

It was the last "KEY TRUTH ADVANTAGE moment" Shannon needed. It was time for her to write her letter and put The Truth Advantage into action.

# Key 7: Live the Truth

Here is the letter she sent:

> Dear Coach,
>
> I'm Shannon Jones, Leanne's mother. You know me as the mom who brings Popsicles to all the girls and cheers very loudly. At the end of each school year, I've always written to the people who have been in Leanne's life to thank them for the lessons they've taught my daughter. Each year, there are different people who have had an effect on Leanne for a variety of reasons.
>
> There are parents who look out for her and tell me how nice she is. I'm thankful for them, glad to know that a few other sets of eyes are looking out for her. There's the guidance counselor who helped her with her college entrance essay and the vice principal who helped her when a bully kept taking her assigned parking space. Other teachers this year have stayed after school to help Leanne in math, given up a lunch hour to go over her Spanish essay, and driven her home when her car broke down. Her field hockey coach has always been inspirational. Did you know she gives out index cards with an inspirational quote on one side and uses the other side to tell players what they're doing great and what they can improve on?
>
> I admit, like probably all the other moms and dads of the daughters you coach, I think my daughter is a star and want her efforts to be encouraged and for her to have every opportunity to fulfill her dreams. I want for the people she encounters in her life to help her realize her talents and reach her fullest potential.
>
> Your coaching decisions have been very hard on Leanne. Instead of encouraging her to play, you've often chosen her as the fall guy, only putting her up to bat in the last inning with one out left. I'm not sure you've thought about just how nervous that might make a young girl who never gets to play. She has come home after several games very upset and feeling like she let her team down.

Besides the week she was out with her tonsils, she has been at each practice, each scrimmage, and at each game, hopefully waiting for her chance to play. I am so proud of Leanne and her dedication and positive attitude. Rather than complaining, she has sat on what we jokingly call "her bucket" without complaint and cheered her teammates on with enthusiasm poise and grace.

I am aware that she asked you once why you weren't letting her play, and, according to her recollection, you told her that you were the coach and you made the decisions. I respect that. You are. So, I'm taking the time to write you this, not to disrespect all you do for our team, but to just make you are aware how it might feel to be the girl on the bucket who never gets picked.

I want to thank you for giving my daughter an important lesson. She now knows that life is sometimes unfair, and though we don't understand why, we have to keep trying. The upside of this season is that although my daughter didn't get to play, she did win. When I told her she could quit, she said, "Mom, I'm not a quitter." She alone made the choice to stay, and she's a much stronger young lady for sticking it out, even when most people would have quit.

I sincerely hope you, as a coach, realize that your actions have a profound effect and everlasting impact on the lives of these young women.

Thank you, Coach, for making my daughter stronger. She will absolutely remember you and this softball season for the rest of her life.

Sincerely,
Shannon Jones, Leanne's mom

## Positive Proof

Do you want to know what happened?

Well, Leanne did indeed win the "Sportsmanship Award," and it was a happy moment for both mother and daughter. But more, my friend Shannon called me recently very excited.

"You're not going to believe it!" she said. "I got a letter back from the coach!" And here is what it said:

Dear Ms. Jones,

Thank you for your letter.
The season is over and so is Leanne's high school career, so I can't go back and put Leanne in the games, but I can tell you that I took your letter to heart. I'm not going to apologize for my coaching decisions, though I will tell you your letter has really made me think about next year and the things I would like to do differently. I may even try the field hockey coach's index card idea. That's a good one.

You have helped me understand an important lesson for coaches and anyone in a position of leadership: Sometimes it's not about winning or losing, it is about letting them get in the game and play. Thank you for taking the time to help me make note of that.

I wish Leanne all future success.

Sincerely,
Coach

Shannon couldn't have been happier if the team were holding the state championship trophy. She had used The Truth Advantage and won.

# Live with The Truth Advantage

Trust is earned. Like money, good grades, and a nice physique, you have to work for it. Practice using the "7 Keys" to deliver your truth, as well as the lie detector to encourage the truth from others, and you will find that your life is indeed happier and more fulfilled.

Remember that The Truth Advantage is more than trying to prove that you're right and someone else is wrong or to deliberately build yourself up and put someone else down. The Truth Advantage happens when you take the opportunity to compassionately communicate your feelings so that you will be listened to, heard, and understood. In return, you'll listen to hear and understand others.

No one expects you to be perfect, but those who know you do wish for all of your encounters with them to be kind. The bottom line is that your words and deeds correlate directly with how well you are liked, respected, and befriended.

As we've seen, there are ways to tell the truth without being hurtful.

To deliver the truth well, you must first learn to communicate with purpose, and that is what each of the "7 Keys to Happiness and Fulfillment" teaches you to do: communicate with others, not manipulate them. When you communicate successfully, you acknowledge the other person's perspective, while conveying yours. When someone knows where you are coming from, he or she is more invested in helping you accomplish what you want to achieve.

**With your children**, ask yourself whether the example you're setting—if they see you twisting or bending the truth—is doing them any favors. Is saving a few bucks by saying they are still young enough to get the "kid's meal" really worth it?

My friend says he learned honesty through playing cards around the kitchen table with his grandfather. When his little kid fingers couldn't grasp all of the cards, and he accidentally exposed his hand, his grandfather would gently remind him to "put some drawers on those cards."

"What's that mean?" he had asked his grandfather the first time he was told this.

"It means honesty is the best policy," his granddad said. "I don't want to beat you because I'm able to see what cards you have in your hand. That wouldn't be the truth. I want to beat you 'fair and square.'" It's a little thing, but here, almost forty years later, my friend remembers it vividly. Be aware that your kids notice and remember. When your children see you telling the truth—even when it's not the easiest choice—you are setting them on a course to live a life filled with integrity and self-respect.

**With your friends and partners**, ask yourself whether you're enjoying a relationship of trust or are you avoiding genuine communication? And, if so, why? What can you do to break that habit and achieve what we all long for—a meaningful connection with others?

Remember, too, there's great power in words and that once they are out, they can't be sucked back in your mouth. Be conscious that your words have weight, and you don't want them to contribute to anyone's already heavy load.

And, hey, let's all work on the lying. It doesn't get you anywhere.

I have a friend who describes herself as "forty-two and voluptuous" on her online dating profile, when she is in fact fifty-seven and chubby. She wonders why she's not getting anywhere with men, why men don't call her after their first date. She thinks there's something wrong with her.

There's nothing wrong with her, she is simply misrepresenting the truth and is doing herself a great disservice. My friend is neither an anomaly in the online dating world nor an anomaly in the real world. Not being truthful is an epidemic. Yet lasting relationships can't be built on lies. It's that simple.

**At work**, say what you mean, mean what you say, always be a person of your word, and you will go far. Being honest at work can build and strengthen relationships with coworkers. I have a friend who works at a software company, and every Friday after work his coworkers all head out to a local bar. These after-hours outings are important professionally, but my friend doesn't drink, so he decided he'd try The Truth Advantage. He told his coworkers that he'd love to go out with them, but that he doesn't drink alcohol. One of his coworkers said, "Then I'll buy you a water! We really want you to come."

He now goes out with them every few weeks—someone "buys" him a water—and he's found that his work life has improved greatly because of the increased camaraderie. By being honest and staying true to himself, he didn't put himself into a situation he's uncomfortable with. He's been surprised that in addition, he's become greatly admired in the office. His coworkers have a newfound respect for his work and his strength of character.

Oh, and if you're going to call out sick, don't post pictures of your day at the beach on your Facebook account. That will get you nowhere. Instead, next time try saying honestly, "I need a day off." You'll find yourself recharged, and you won't have to hide your tan.

**In dealing with lies and liars,** remember that people often lie out of fear: fear of conflict, fear of rejection, fear of punishment, and fear of loss. Here's how to use the "7 Keys" to encourage those you know to be honest with you:

1. **Look in the mirror:** Encourage the person you're speaking with to make his or her own self-examination. When my children are not being their best selves, I always ask them, "Is this the you, you want to be?"

2. **Listen up:** When you tell people that you've caught them in a lie, you should be open to hearing what they have to say in response. Don't close down; be receptive.

3. **Get your facts straight:** There is nothing worse than being wrongly accused. Before you confront anyone—accusing him or her of being dishonest—make sure you've double-checked your information. Just as none of us like to be lied to, it's horrible to be wrongly accused of lying.

4. **Time it right:** It's a good idea to simply let the person know that something has been troubling you and then

negotiate a mutually agreeable time and place to sit down in a peaceful, low-key setting that will be comfortable for both of you. You don't want to call someone out on your cell phone, and you don't want your friend to receive your statement right after she's gotten a root canal. Choosing the right time and place will set your conversation up for success.

5. **Think it through:** You're ready to say what you feel, but be prepared to come from the right place and for the right reason. Confronting someone who has lied to you is a very difficult, tense thing to do. You'll want to have thought through what you're going to say. You'll have the most success going in if you know to keep your anger to a minimum and your harsh words under lock and key.

6. **Admit your mistakes:** I always begin a difficult conversation by admitting that it's a difficult conversation. Own up to where you're coming from and say that you're hurt, confused, or angry.

7. **Live the truth:** When you're dealing with a lie, the best course of action is the truth. Think about why the person might have lied. It may have been out of the need to protect him- or herself, to avoid punishment, as a response to fear, or as a way to get attention. Explain how you care for the individual and want to have a great relationship.

CHAPTER 15

# Truth: A Very Important Issue

*A half truth is a whole lie.*

—YIDDISH PROVERB

In December 2006, the *Merriam-Webster Dictionary* announced that its "Word of the Year" had been selected. Given the previous years' words and discussions surrounding their selection, the "Word of the Year" had gained a following of enthralled linguists, both young and old, with varied interests and backgrounds. Like *Time* magazine's Person of the Year, Major League Baseball's Rookie of the Year, and the supermodel adorning the cover of the *Sport's Illustrated* Swimsuit Edition, the "Word of the Year" had become a pop culture icon.

When America's dictionary publisher began the "Word of the Year" in 2003, the Word had been determined by an analysis of page hits and searches on its online dictionary website. The most popular word won. From 2003 to 2005, each of the words correlated to big news stories and world events. In short, the Word of the Year gained the reputation of being a current events barometer, something that defined the time. In 2003, the word was *democracy*. It was connected to the invasion of Iraq and the overthrow of Saddam Hussein's regime. In 2004, the word was *blog*. No surprise there. Blogs were popping up on the Web faster than weeds in the spring, and these citizen journalists had begun to influence even mainstream media. In 2005, the word was *integrity*. *Merriam-Webster* said the word had slowly moved to first position after a series of ethics scandals in America regarding corporations, government, and sports figures.

Then, in 2006, *Merriam-Webster* announced that it was going to select the Word of the Year a little differently. This time, *Merriam-Webster* decided to post an online poll to select twenty words as finalists. Visitors to the site would then vote for the winning word that they thought defined the year. So, in 2006 the word was chosen by popular opinion.

When it came time for the announcement, Merriam-Webster said that the 2006 Word of the Year had beaten *google*, the second-place word on the list, by a dramatic 5 to 1 margin. Shocking, considering that we were all "googling" to find everything from news to information about our potential dates. So, what was the word that year? The word was *truthiness*, defined as "a 'truth' that a person claims to know intuitively 'from the gut' without regard to evidence, logic, intellectual examination, or facts." *Truthiness* had been used satirically on the first episode of television comedian Stephen Colbert's *Colbert Report* to describe things that he fervently believed in, regardless of the facts. At the end of his performance, Colbert had said, "I know some of you may not trust your gut, yet. But with my help, you will. The truthiness is, anyone can read the news to you. I promise to feel the news 'at' you."

*Merriam-Webster* gave *truthiness* two definitions: "truth that comes from the gut, not books" and "the quality of preferring concepts or facts one wishes to be true, rather than concepts of facts known to be true." John Morse, *Merriam-Webster*'s president, said, "We're at a point where what constitutes truth is a question on a lot of people's minds, and truth has come up for grabs. 'Truthiness' is a playful way for us to think about a very important issue."

"Truth has come up for grabs." Wow. Have we arrived at a spot where we've bought the bull for so long that we can no longer tell the difference between true and false? Is dishonesty an unstoppable epidemic? Should we just accept that truth is now passé, like last season's fashions? Has life become so filled with contradictions, misperceptions, and shell games that we're now numbed and apathetic to reality? Have we arrived at a time and a place where we all just expect to be lied to? Or, as Leonard Cohen wrote in *My Secret Life*, "I smile when I'm angry, I cheat and I lie. I do what I have to do to get by. But I know what is wrong and I know what is right, and I'd die for the truth in my secret life."

A friend who is a college professor told me that the dishonesty and outright deception she has been observing in her students is not only disheartening, it is nothing short of frightening. "I'm alarmed by the way a student can come to me after class, look me right in the eye, and lie. Just last week, a student came to my office to explain that she missed the exam the day before because she was in the emergency room. She rather pompously handed over a note from the hospital, which did say she had been in the emergency room for stomach cramps. When I pointed out it was for the week before, she just looked at me and smiled."

I remember in college being a student representative on the Honor Code Board and meeting a young woman who had plagiarized and cheated on papers and exams. More than simply denying what she had done, she expressed outrage that she had even been accused. The problem for her was that the teacher and the other students had caught the cheating, and the plagiarism was literally word for word. I marveled at how she didn't understand that she had lied. In her mind, she must have truly believed she was telling the truth.

Have we parents dropped the ball in teaching right and wrong to our kids, or are we all now just complicit players in one big con game? Each day, are we just trying to get by and get away with what we can? And do we let people get away with lying to us because we simply don't care?

It's hard to deny that integrity and honesty in our modern world are in short supply. We are living in what has become a "me" culture. Too many people seem to be practitioners of the school of thought that the end justifies the means, that as long as it works out for "me, me, me," it's okay. But if it were just you and you, would you want you to lie to you? Probably not. You'd probably want you to tell you the truth.

I recently attended a dinner party where a guest was bemoaning that it seemed like we had become a *"Survivor* society," where the object of the game is to "outwit, outplay, outlast." In this game, the person who dies with the most toys wins, regardless of how he or she lied and cheated to get there. His wife spoke up to say that she'd decided that humans weren't the superior species—dogs were. "They don't lie," she laughed. "They may lay. But they don't lie." Everyone laughed with her, and then there was an awkward silence as we each sipped our soup.

**Communication professor.** Dr. Mark L. Knapp, the author of *Lying and Deception in Human Interaction*, told me that if we continue to believe "the idea that truth is elusive or can't be known, so you don't need to concern yourself with it," we're in trouble. He says the thought that "everybody else is lying so why shouldn't I?" is damaging. Simply put, it is self-destructive to think that because everyone else is being dishonest, you can and should be, too.

The fact that you're holding this book in your hands is the first step in saying you've had enough. You want change. And you believe that change can start with you.

Daniel Craven, the author of *The Guide to Honest Parenting*, believes that without a move toward truth, civilization, as we know it, will crumble. "As an ingredient in society," he said, "truth obviously has as much value as food and water. Truth is the foundation of any relationship, from a spouse to your postal delivery person. Choosing whether or not to use honesty with colleagues, clients, and contacts will help to make or break a career. Raising our children with or without it will make or break our world."

Psychiatrist Dale Archer agrees. "If you don't have trust," he told me, "you don't have a relationship." And, if you're like me, you are seeking solid relationships with the people in your life. You want to feel as if you really know those you associate with, and you want them to really know you. Otherwise, to put it bluntly, what's the point?

"Keeping secrets and not being honest builds walls between people and stops the flow of sharing, spontaneity, and intimacy," said Dr. Margaret Paul, the creator of the "Inner Bonding" relationship technique. "In addition, keeping secrets and avoiding telling each other things is a form of control, so it stops the learning and growth that are vital for a loving relationship."

None of us wants a life of "truthiness." We want the truth. As humans, none of us can ever be as perfect as we want to be. Yet the goal of The Truth Advantage is to first help you recognize the benefits of having integrity and being truthful and then using the 7 Keys to climb that mountain and grasp those qualities, rather than continuing to slide away from them. We must strive to acknowledge and accept our own personal flaws, our individual failures at being truthful, and work toward achieving honest communication, which will fertilize an organic improvement of ourselves and our lives. Though we are often affected, bothered, and disappointed by others' lack of integrity, in order to bring about change, we must first begin with personal growth. It starts with each of us.

"To me, truth is not some vague, foggy notion," Jack Handey said. "Truth is real. And, at the same time, unreal. Fiction and fact and everything in between, plus some things I can't remember, all rolled into one big 'thing.' This is truth, to me."

Let's go back to the very basics: what is truth, really? When we started it seemed like such an easy word, didn't it? How does the *Merriam-Webster Dictionary* actually define *truth*?

1. *a archaic*: fidelity, constancy *b*: sincerity in action, character, and utterance

2. a (1): the state of being the case: fact (2): the body of real things, events, and facts: actuality (3) *often capitalized*: a transcendent fundamental or spiritual reality b: a judgment, proposition, or idea that is true or accepted as true.

*Fidelity and constancy.* I'd guess that if you're anything like me, you want that, right? Certainly, none of us is begging to be with someone who is erratic, unfaithful, or disloyal, whether it is a friend, a partner, or colleague. And we surely don't want these qualities in our children!

*Sincerity in action, character, and utterance.* I definitely aspire to be sincere in my actions and for people to be sincere with me. Who would ever ask for or desire insincerity? I personally want people around me to be genuine, and even if they are "characters," I want them to be of good character. I want to know that they'd never intentionally do me wrong, hurt me, or say things about me that weren't true. I'm also sure that's the friend you'd want to both be and have.

*The state of being the case: fact.* It's hard to argue with facts. I learned this in elementary school and practiced it in the courtroom. Facts are truths that are hard to argue. The earth is round. Fact. Two plus two equals four. Fact. A red light means stop. Fact. When you have the facts, you have the truth.

*A transcendent fundamental or spiritual reality.* This is Truth with a capital T, our spiritual quest to find higher meaning and our reason for being.

*A judgment, proposition, or idea that is true or accepted as true.* Now, here's where we've got a horse race. A "judgment" brings in a certain subjective element. For example, if I were to say, "Oh, that dress is beautiful!" am I suggesting that everyone thinks it is beautiful, that the entire world would agree with me? No. But I'm stating my personal truth, my own judgment or idea about that dress. In my honest opinion, it is beautiful.

Admittedly, the truth is not always cut and dried, because an opinion, even though it is your truthful opinion, is different from an absolute truth supported by inarguable fact. Telling a friend you crashed his computer is not the same as telling him you don't like his girlfriend. One is a fact; the other is a more subjective truth, your estimation. Your view may be that his girlfriend is dumber than a box of rocks, meaner than a snake, and uglier than a burnt stump, but whether you like her or not is your opinion, and unless asked, you might just be better off keeping that opinion to yourself. (Incidentally, the truth is the girlfriend might not like you, either.)

The great Oscar Wilde said, "The pure and simple truth is rarely pure and never simple."

So, as you embark to use the 7 Keys and gain The Truth Advantage, think of truth as a ladder, simple facts are the most basic, lowest rungs, and spiritual truths are the highest rung. Between the two is the truth that often makes us run and hide.

The easiest of truths to say and grasp are the simplest, such as "Can you have lunch on Tuesday?" and "Is tomorrow Thursday or Friday?" These are truths that we can answer quickly and honestly with little or no consequence. When opinion comes into play, the truth becomes a little more difficult because our egos get involved. We suddenly worry whether someone might question our tastes or preferences. For example, "Do you like this color?" My opinion may be affected by your opinion. Before I answer, I may try to read you, take a temperature for your attitude toward the color. This can happen for a variety of reasons: perhaps I don't want to hurt your feelings, maybe I don't want you to think I have bad taste, or I might not want to tell you I'm color blind.

Dr. Mark L. Knapp told me, "I believe we should try to tell the truth as often as we can, but I also realize that some situations may call for something short of that. Everything changes with time, so why wouldn't we expect our view of honesty to change?"

Up the truth ladder a rung or two are simple truths that might make us a little uncomfortable, whether we're on the speaking end or the receiving end. I chuckled at a recent question posed on PollDaddy.com. The site asked its users about a simple truth, "Do you want to be told if there's something in your teeth after a meal?" An astounding 99 percent of respondents said they would absolutely want to be told, including 5 percent who hoped a close friend would be there to tell them. Less than 1 percent said that they would rather not be told, because the truth would have been too embarrassing. To that tiny minority, I ask, So, you think it's not embarrassing to go through the rest of your day with a big piece of spinach dangling between your front teeth?

Then, there are truths that are tougher to tell, possibly because they're harder to hear. "You've gained a little weight." "You're not qualified for the job." "You can't sing." None of us wants to hear that we're fat. None of us wants to hear that we're not qualified. None of us wants to think we lack talent. For those reasons, these truths are harder to deliver. We know they are not what the recipients want to hear. No matter how many times the judges on *American Idol* tell wannabe-stars they're not singers, it doesn't make it easier to witness as a viewer or hear as a contestant. Yet truths such as these, though uncomfortable, can be tools to genuinely motivate someone toward a better path, so long as they are spoken from the right place. As a high school runner in the mile, I was pretty darned good and even broke some records in Washington State, but I was never going to be Olympic caliber. Even though it hurt me to hear that from my coach, it actually freed me to concentrate on my studies and get into a good college.

As we climb the ladder, and face the world with truth, the toughest rungs are at the top. These are truths that are difficult to say and often painful to accept because they involve things that are fundamental to our individual identities. "I'm gay." "I cheated." Or "I don't love you anymore." These truths, often the most emotional, are also sometimes the most beneficial to personal growth and mental health.

When I was a little girl, a pinky swear between friends was the highest and most revered of adolescent covenants. Oh, how times have changed. I recently saw a cartoon that depicted two little girls standing on a playground. One of the little girls has a gentleman standing next to her holding a briefcase. The little girl says to her friend, "Sorry, but pinky swear doesn't cut it anymore. My attorney has a few documents for you to sign." We laugh. That's funny. But it's funny because we are almost there!

Listen to people as you go about your day. Be aware of what people say and how they say it. We've become such a society of fibbers that we often have to amend something we're saying with a "this is the truth" modifier: "Let me be honest." Oh, so you haven't been honest with me up until now? "Here's the truth." Oh, has the rest of the stuff you've been saying been a load of bull? "Honestly." As opposed to? Because lying has become second nature, do we now have to modify our important statements so that the listener will know that this part is absolutely true? Perhaps we have to swear to it and then concentrate real hard!

The United States is known to have one of the most respected judicial systems in the world. Each year, millions of people—from judges to jurors, the accused to their accusers—participate in this system, which is established to settle disputes and seek justice for all. I've worked in the law for fifteen years of my life, eight as a practicing attorney and seven as a law professor. Watching people take the oath and swear to tell the truth was one of the most fascinating of experiences.

You probably know the courtroom oath: "I swear to tell the whole truth and nothing but the truth." There is a reason that you are asked in court to tell the whole truth. It's because for most of our daily lives this is not what people do. People lie for many reasons, sometimes for their own advantage, other times not. But being reminded to tell the truth, that you've sworn to tell the truth, gives people pause. Our justice system wouldn't work without that oath. There is only one thing that matters in the courtroom—not who your parents are, your car, your education, but only the truth. Court is a reflection of our societal values, and when liberty is at stake, the one thing we are asked is to tell the truth.

The very first legal systems were founded on people swearing to tell the truth before God. The subtext being, if you didn't tell the truth, God would punish you. If you lied, you risked eternal damnation. Today, most courts have done away with the swearing on a Bible and the reference to God, but not without question and consequence. Devout people feel that the removal of God from the courtroom oath is an attack on religion. Many suggest that without a vow before God, there will be no moral consequence, and people will readily lie. Even nonbelievers might be more inclined to believe someone who puts his or her soul on the line before the Almighty.

I heard a story of a courtroom swearing-in incident in which the witness, an elderly lady, paused after the bailiff read, "Do you swear to tell the whole truth and nothing but the truth?" The woman sat on the witness stand quietly for a few seconds, and the bailiff asked, "Do you?" The witness said, "Oh, I do, but I'm waiting for 'so help me God.'" The judge told the woman she could add "so help me God," and the woman raised her right hand, repeated the oath, and ended with a dramatic "so help me God." Here's what I know about that scene and the woman's testimony: no matter what the jurors' backgrounds, beliefs, and ideologies, the woman was instantly trusted. She was willing to say it wasn't only perjury she was worried about. She was laying her soul on the line that she was telling the truth before God.

As we've already noted, lying is commonplace today. It's not necessarily that we're all walking around intentionally dealing out big whoppers, but rather that people tell little lies every day. It's become a societal norm. So why should we expect someone to arrive in court and suddenly tell the truth? How do we get people to tell the truth on the witness stand? Well, we threaten them with punishment. In your day-to-day life, lying might cost you a friend or a job, but if you're caught lying in court, you can go to jail.

The truth is the one thing that is expected—demanded—of everyone who takes the witness stand in the courtroom. The necessary rule that keeps our court system working is that if you are testifying, whatever comes out of your mouth must be the truth, whether it be about a traffic accident, a divorce case, or first-degree murder. The ramifications for not telling the truth—committing perjury—are very serious. Just ask Martha Stewart.

As I've often said, the cover-up is worse than the crime. Martha Stewart did not go to jail because of her well-timed sale of ImClone stock but because she told a lie to cover up a $45,000 profit. Here's how it happened. After getting a call from her broker's assistant telling her that the CEO of ImClone was unloading all of his stock ahead of a Food and Drug Administration rejection of the company's new cancer drug, Stewart sold nearly four thousand shares of her stock in the company. When asked about the trade, she said she had an agreement with her broker that he would sell her shares once the price dropped below $60 a share.

Her mistake was that lie. She thought that her reputation would enable her to get away with it. She was convicted of obstructing justice, conspiracy, and making false statements. Before her sentencing, she wrote the judge a four-page letter and asked him to "consider all the good that I have done, all the contributions I have made, and all the intense suffering that has accompanied every single moment of the past two and a half years." All of that good she had done did nothing for her once she was caught in a lie. And it cost her way more than five months of jail time and a $30,000 fine. It cost Stewart her reputation, the chairmanship of her company, and a chunk of her fortune.

Dr. Mark L. Knapp explains it this way: "Deliberate falsehoods, when uncovered, are normally sanctioned more than attempts to avoid or hedge the truth."

But why can't people learn? President Richard Nixon should have been a lesson to us all. Watergate, the political scandal he had attempted to cover up, ultimately forced him to resign from office. We as a nation witnessed his fall and watched his lies take him down, yet we still think that only other people get caught and that we'll skate on by. And why is this? Perhaps because most people in our lives allow us to skate on by.

When I was a prosecutor, I never put witnesses on the stand without giving them my "truth speech." I told them that I wanted the truth, expected the truth, and that I could deal with anything as long as they told me the truth. I told them they would be okay unless they lied, which, not surprisingly, is the exact same thing I tell my teenage kids, Jacob and Dani. Sure, there can be a punishment if you do something wrong, but if you lie and get caught intentionally hiding the truth, the outcome will be a lot worse.

So, do people lie in court? Yes, I had people lie to me all of the time. But one of the problems with lying on the witness stand is that you almost always get caught. Why? Because it is nearly impossible to keep track of your lies when there's a long barrage of pointed questions coming your way that you have to answer. In your personal life, your friends might let you slide without further questioning if, for example, you say you can't go to dinner because of a previous engagement. On the witness stand, you're asked all about the previous engagement. Details. In the courtroom, you don't have a benevolent group of friends letting you pass; you have a judge and a jury, as well as an opposing side. And let it be known that attorneys are paid handsomely to get to the truth. This is also a good time to point out that if testimony goes into the record and is later revealed to be a lie, it's not only the witness who is in trouble. The side he's testifying for is, too, because they've just lost all credibility.

Similarly, even if your friends aren't billboarding your lies or calling you out on them, trust me, they are on to you. And once you've gone down that path, once you've lost credibility, it's very hard to get it back. Everything you say is taken with a grain of salt. No, your friends won't cry "perjury." They probably won't try to lock you up. But they will look to another person when they need someone to trust.

Would you want your doctor to lie to you? How about your car mechanic? What about your child's teacher? Of course not! And they wouldn't want you to lie to them. We must hold ourselves to that same high standard. I've never had a high tolerance for lies or liars, but while working on this book, I've been thinking of myself as being on the witness stand. I've woken up each morning and sworn to tell the truth, and what I've found is that when I'm telling the truth and expecting it from others, everything in my life has been better—from my personal to my professional encounters.

A truthful person is an authentic person. It's been said for millennia, but let it be said again: the truth shall set you free. If you want to relieve your stress, transform your life, and really get ahead, you'll learn to tell the truth. When people are telling the truth, they are freed from the burden, the guilt, and the energy it takes to keep up with lies. They are happier and healthier. It is downright refreshing to be with someone who is honest, swimming against the tide of moral mud. We want to be around people who are striving to be real in the morass of our "reality show" world.

Honesty is valued for a reason, because it demonstrates a sense of morality and ethics. Lying has consequences for both the liar and those affected. (Just ask anyone who trusted a man named Bernie Madoff!) The truth matters because we all want to believe that what is being said to us and what we are seeing is reality. We want criminals punished for their bad behavior and our heroes to be appropriately rewarded. With those we know and love, we seek relationships of understanding, honesty, and truth or, as the *Merriam-Webster Dictionary* defines it, "fidelity, constancy, and sincerity in action, character, and utterance."

Truth is necessary for forging genuine relationships, for effectively communicating with the people in our lives, and for making our homes, our careers, and our society stable and secure. As psychologist Dr. Leon Seltzer noted in his *Psychology Today* blog, "Daily I look around me and observe how people shy away from genuine, self-revealing communication—almost as though to embark on such a path would be like walking into a minefield, where a single misstep might be fatal." Without becoming more honest in our daily lives, we will slowly but surely diminish our ability to connect with those who mean the most to us.

Truth isn't a luxury. It's a necessity.

# Final Thoughts

L et's come back to where we started. You are you. Only you
know who you want to be, where you want to go, and how
you want to get there. I hope this book has shown you that the
truthful course is the best course for you and the world. Because
in the end, as Abraham Lincoln so wisely observed, "You can
fool all of the people some of the time, and some of the people
all the time, but you cannot fool all of the people all the time."

Yes, honesty and integrity are sorely lacking in modern
times. Many of our leaders are no longer held in esteem. The
more our celebrities lack virtue, the more attention they get.
Even some of our religious leaders are getting by with a "Do as
I say, not as I do" standard. The people whom we've been
taught to admire, to look up to, to aspire to be have often failed
to meet our high expectations.

So, what do we do to turn the tide on this wave of dishonesty?

You now know what to do. You have the "7 Keys." Use them, and, as Confucius said, "Wheresover you go, go with all your heart."

Become the wonderful, truthful person you'd want to have as a friend, a colleague, a loved one.

In short, it's up to each of us. We each must live the truth.

Now, go forward and achieve your most happy and fulfilled life with The Truth Advantage.

# Index